OLD TESTAMENT STORIES

D0702066

Published by
The Church of Jesus Christ of Latter-day Saints
Salt Lake City, Utah

TABLE OF CONTENTS

INTRODUCTION

To the Reader

This book will help you read and understand some of the stories from the Old Testament. These stories are taken from a book that is sacred. As you read these stories, remember they are about real people who lived long ago.

Read the stories over and over until you know them well. You will also want to read them from the Bible. Under each picture you will see where you can find that story in the Bible. Have your father, mother, teacher, or friend help you.

If you do not know a word, look it up in "Words to Know" at the back of the book. If you do not know a person or place, look it up in "People to Know" or "Places to Know" at the back of the book.

To Parents and Teachers

This book will help you teach the scriptures. The "Words to Know," "People to Know," and "Places to Know" sections and the maps will help you teach the meanings of words in this book and the identity of Old Testament people and places.

As you teach, share your testimony of the Bible. Encourage those whom you teach to seek prayerfully their own testimonies. Their understanding will grow when you read to them their favorite stories from the Bible itself.

If you are using this volume to teach the handicapped, you may be encouraged by the words of the Prophet Joseph Smith: "All the minds and spirits that God ever sent into the world are susceptible of enlargement" (*Teachings of the Prophet Joseph Smith,* sel. by Joseph Fielding Smith [Salt Lake City: Deseret Book Company, 1938] p. 354).

BEFORE THE
OLD TESTAMENT

CHAPTER 1

God lives in heaven. He is our Heavenly Father. We lived in heaven with him. We lived with him a long time. He taught us many things.

Matthew 6:9; D&C 93:29;

In heaven we did not have flesh-and-blood bodies. We had spirit bodies. Our spirit bodies looked like the flesh and blood bodies we have now. We were the spirit children of God.

Hebrews 12:9; D&C 77:2; Abraham 3:22

One day Heavenly Father talked to all his children. He said he would make an earth for us. He said we could go to earth. He said we must go to get flesh and blood bodies.

Abraham 3:23-24; Hebrews 2:14

God said we would be *tested* on earth. We should obey his commandments. But God would not make us obey him. We could choose. We would come back to heaven and live with God if we obeyed him.

Abraham 3:26; D&C 29:36-39

God chose some spirits to help him on earth. They were righteous. He knew they would obey his commandments. They would be prophets and leaders.

Abraham 3:23

God said one of his sons would save the people on the earth. He would go to earth and die for all of us. God's son, Jesus Christ, said *he* would go to earth and die for us. He would obey God.

Alma 22:13; Abraham 3:27, Moses 4:2

Then another son spoke. His name was Lucifer. He said he would go to earth. But he wanted God's power. God chose Jesus Christ. Lucifer was angry.

Moses 4:1; D&C 29:36; Abraham 3:28

Lucifer talked to God's children. He wanted us to obey him. He said he would make us be good. We could not choose. He would bring us all back to heaven.

Moses 4:1, 3

Many spirits followed Lucifer. Lucifer and these spirits did not obey God.

D&C 29:36-37

God was very sad. He sent Lucifer and the spirits who followed Lucifer out of heaven. They could not have flesh-and-blood bodies. They could not go back to heaven. Lucifer would lead them. His name would be Satan or the devil.

D&C 76:25-27; D&C 29:37; Revelation 12:9

JESUS MAKES THE EARTH

CHAPTER 2

It was time to make the earth. Heavenly Father chose Jesus Christ to make it. He told Jesus how to make it. Jesus made the earth in six days.

The days were much longer than our days. The first day Jesus made the light. He called it day. He made the dark. He called it night.

3 Nephi 9:15; Genesis 1:7-26; 2 Peter 3:8

The second day Jesus divided the water. Some water was on the earth. Some water was in the clouds in the sky.

Genesis 1:7

The third day Jesus made dry land. He made the grass and the trees grow. He made all the plants grow.

Genesis 1:9-13

The fourth day Jesus made the sun. He made
the moon and the stars.

Genesis 1:14-19

The fifth day Jesus put fish in the water. He also made the birds. The sixth day Jesus made all the other animals. He made cows and horses and dogs. He made deer and lions and tigers.

Genesis 1:20-25

God and Jesus made a man. He was the first man on earth. His name was Adam. Adam looked like God and Jesus. Adam lived in a beautiful garden. It was called the Garden of Eden.

Genesis 1:26-31; Genesis 2:7-8

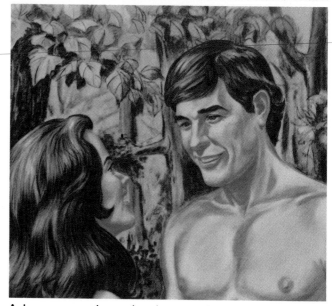

Adam was alone in the garden. So God and Jesus made a woman. Her name was Eve. She was Adam's wife.

Genesis 2:20-25; Genesis 3:20

God and Jesus told Adam and Eve to take care of the garden. They told them to have children.

Genesis 1:28

God and Jesus looked at all they had made. It was good. On the seventh day they rested.

Genesis 1:31; Genesis 2:1-3

ADAM AND EVE

CHAPTER 3

Adam and Eve lived in the Garden of Eden. God and Jesus came and talked to them. There were many trees in the garden. God said Adam and Eve could eat fruit from all the trees but one.

Genesis 3:8; 2:16-17

It was the tree of good and evil. If they ate fruit from that tree, they would know what was good and what was bad. They would have to leave the Garden of Eden. If they did not eat it, they could always stay in the Garden of Eden. God said they could choose.

Genesis 2:16-17; Moses 3:17

One day Satan, the devil, came to the Garden of Eden. He told Eve she should eat the fruit of the tree of good and evil. Eve said God had told her and Adam not to eat it.

Genesis 3:1-3

Satan said the fruit was very good. He told Eve it would make her wise. She would know good and evil. Eve chose to eat the fruit.

Genesis 3:4-6

Eve told Adam she had eaten the fruit. She would have to leave the garden. She gave Adam some of the fruit. Adam ate it.

Genesis 3:6-7

God came to see Adam and Eve. They had not obeyed God. They were afraid. They ran and hid.

Genesis 3:8

God talked to Adam and Eve. He asked if they had eaten the fruit of good and evil. They said Satan told them to eat it. So they ate the fruit.

Genesis 3:9-13

God told Adam and Eve they must leave the garden of Eden. They could not live there any more. Adam and Eve left the garden of Eden.

Genesis 3:16-24

Adam and Eve worked hard to get food. They grew older. They knew they would die someday.

Genesis 3:16, 19; Moses 5:1

Adam and Eve knew good and evil. They had children. Sometimes they were happy. Sometimes they were sad.

Genesis 4:1; Moses 5:2, 11

God gave Adam and Eve commandments. He said they should pray to him. God told Adam to make sacrifices to him. To make a sacrifice, Adam killed an animal. He burned the animal on an altar of stone.

Moses 5:4-5

An angel came to Adam. He said Jesus would sacrifice his life for us someday. It would be his gift to us. The sacrifices helped Adam and Eve think about the sacrifice of Jesus.

Moses 5:6-8

ADAM AND HIS FAMILY

CHAPTER 4

Adam and Eve had many children. They had a son named Cain. He worked in the fields. He loved Satan more than he loved God.

Genesis 5:4; Moses 5:16-18; Genesis 4:1-2

Adam and Eve had another son, named Abel. Abel took care of the sheep. He obeyed God's commandments.

Genesis 4:2-4

Cain was wicked. He was angry at God and Abel. One day Cain and Abel were in the fields. Satan told Cain to kill Abel. Then Cain killed his brother Abel.

Genesis 4:5-8

God knew Cain had killed Abel. He asked Cain where Abel was. Cain told a lie. He said he did not know.

God said he knew what Cain had done. Cain said Satan had told him to kill Abel. God said Cain would be punished for killing his brother.

Genesis 4:9-12; Moses 5:34-38

Cain could not be with God any more. Cain and his wife went to live in another place. Some of Cain's brothers went with them.

Genesis 4:16; Moses 5:41

Cain and his brothers had large families. They did not obey God's commandments. They became very wicked.

Genesis 4:17-24; Moses 5:42-55

Seth was one of Adam and Eve's sons. Seth was a good man. He taught his children to love God. He taught them to read and write. They had the priesthood. The priesthood is the power of God.

Genesis 4:25-26; Moses 6:2-7

Many years passed. Many people lived on the earth. Satan told the people to do wicked things.

Most of the people obeyed Satan. God was not happy with them.

Genesis 6:1-6

ENOCH

Enoch was a prophet. He was a righteous man. He was filled with the Holy Ghost. The Holy Ghost helped him.

Moses 6:21, 23, 26, 38

Most of the people on earth were wicked. They did not believe in God. God was angry with them.

Moses 6:27-28

God talked to Enoch. God said he would bless Enoch. He would give Enoch power to teach the people. Enoch should tell the people to repent. They should obey God's commandments.

Moses 6:27-34

Enoch taught in many places. He told the people they were wicked. They should repent. God would punish them if they did not repent. Enoch spoke with the power of God. The people were afraid.

Moses 6:27-29; 37-39; Moses 7:13

Enoch said Jesus Christ would come to earth. He would suffer for the sins of the people. If they were righteous and were baptized, they could live in heaven again.

Moses 6:57-59

Some of the people repented and became righteous. God told Enoch to baptize them. God blessed the righteous people.

Moses 7:11, 17

Enoch led the righteous people. Enoch built a city and named it Zion. The righteous people lived in Zion.

Moses 7:19

23

Enoch had a vision. God showed him all the people on earth. Enoch saw the people in his city go to heaven.

Moses 7:21

The wicked people stayed on earth. God said he would send a flood to earth. The wicked people would die in the water. Only Noah and his family would be saved.

Moses 7:28, 32-36, 43

Enoch saw everything that would happen on earth. He saw Jesus Christ die on the cross. Then he saw Jesus go up to heaven.

Moses 7:45, 55-57, 59

Enoch saw Jesus come back to earth in the last days. Then the wicked people suffered. The righteous people were blessed. Enoch saw all these things in his vision.

Moses 7:60-67

God came to the city of Zion many times. Then God took Enoch and all the people in Zion to heaven.

Moses 7:68-69; Genesis 5:24

NOAH

CHAPTER 6

Many years passed. Most of the people on earth were wicked. But Noah and his three sons were righteous. They obeyed God's commandments. Noah had the priesthood.

Genesis 6:5, 9-10; Moses 8:13, 19, 27

God was very sad because the people were wicked.

Genesis 6:6

God told Noah to tell the people to repent. He would send a flood to the earth.

Moses 8:19; Genesis 6:17

Noah told the people to repent. He told them to believe in Jesus Christ. He told them to be baptized. Then the Holy Ghost would help them.

The wicked people did not listen to Noah. They did not repent. They tried to kill Noah.

Moses 8:20, 23-24, 26

God said all the wicked people on earth would die in the flood. Most of the animals would die. But Noah and his family would not die.

Genesis 6:17-21

God told Noah to build a big ship. It was called an ark. Noah and his sons obeyed God. They built the ark. The ark had many rooms. It had a window and a door on the side.

Genesis 6:14-16, 22

Noah and his sons put food in the ark. Two animals of every kind came to Noah. God told Noah to put them in the ark.

Genesis 6:21-22; 7:8-9

Noah and his family went into the ark. Rain began to fall. It rained for 40 days and 40 nights. The water covered the earth. The wicked people died in the flood.

Genesis 7:12-23

Noah's family was safe on the ark. God blessed them.

Genesis 7:23; 8:1

At last the rain stopped. The water stayed on the earth for a long time. Then the water went down. The ark landed on a high mountain. The land became dry again.

Genesis 8:2-5, 14

Noah took his family and the animals out of the ark.

Genesis 8:18-19

Noah thanked God for saving their lives. He built an altar. He burned sacrifices. God promised Noah he would never again send a flood to cover the earth. God put a rainbow in the sky. The rainbow helps people remember God's promise to Noah.

Genesis 8:20-22; 9:8-17

THE TOWER OF BABEL

After the flood Noah's sons had many children. Their children grew up and had families. There were many people on the earth again. Some of them built a city.

Genesis 10; Genesis 11:4

The people wanted to build a tall tower. They wanted to climb the tower to go to heaven. It was called the Tower of Babel.

Genesis 11:4, 9

People cannot climb a tower to go to heaven. People must obey God to go to heaven. God saw the people building the tower.

Genesis 11:5

God did not want the people to build the tower. He changed the language of the people. Each one spoke words the others did not know. The people could not talk to each other.

Genesis 11:7

They could not work together. They could not finish the tower. They left the city.

Genesis 11:9

Jared and his brother lived near the tower. They were righteous men. They loved God and obeyed him.

Ether 1:33-34

The brother of Jared prayed to God. He asked God not to change their language. They wanted to talk to their families.

Ether 1:35-37

God blessed them. He let them keep their language.

Ether 1:35, 37

These people were called the Jaredites. They went to America. The Book of Mormon tells about the Jaredites.

Ether

ABRAHAM

CHAPTER 8

Abraham was a righteous man. He lived in the city of Ur.

Abraham 1:1-2; 2:1; Genesis 11:31

Sarah was Abraham's wife. They had no children.

Genesis 11:29-30

Other people in Ur prayed to idols. They did not obey God. They killed some righteous people. They tried to kill Abraham.

Abraham 1:5, 7, 11-12

Abraham prayed. God said he would bless Abraham and his family. God would send a famine to the wicked people. There would be no food.

Abraham 1:15, 29

God told Abraham and Sarah to leave Ur. He would lead them to the promised land. They obeyed God.

Abraham 2:3-6

God sent the famine. There was no food.

Abraham 2:21

Abraham and Sarah traveled to find food. There was food in the land of Egypt.

Abraham 2:21; Genesis 12:10

Abraham and Sarah went to Egypt. The king of Egypt liked them. He gave them many gifts and animals. They became rich.

Genesis 12:15-16; 13:2

Later Abraham and Sarah left Egypt. They took their animals with them. They traveled a long time.

Genesis 13:1-3

At last they came to the promised land. God told Abraham to look at the land. God gave him the land.

Genesis 13:14, 17

Many years passed. There were wars in the land. Abraham took his servants to fight. They won the war.

Genesis 14:14-16

After the war Abraham met Melchizedek. Melchizedek was a righteous king. He had the priesthood. He blessed Abraham.

Genesis 14:18-19

Abraham paid his tithing to Melchizedek.

Genesis 14:20

God said Abraham's family would be large. His family would have the priesthood. His family could have the promised land.

Genesis 17:4-8

Abraham and Sarah were sad because they had no children.

Genesis 15:2-3

Later God said Abraham and Sarah would have a son. His name would be Isaac. He would serve God and obey his commandments. Sarah was 90 years old. She was too old to have a baby. But God said Sarah would have a baby.

Genesis 17:15-21

ABRAHAM AND THE SACRIFICE OF ISAAC

CHAPTER 9

Sarah had a baby boy named Isaac.

Genesis 21:1-3

God wanted to know if Abraham would obey him. God told him to sacrifice Isaac on a mountain.

Genesis 22:1-2

Abraham loved his son very much. He did not want to sacrifice Isaac. But Abraham wanted to obey God.

Genesis 22:2-3

God told Abraham to go to a mountain. He took Isaac and two men with him. Abraham and Isaac rode on a donkey. They traveled for three days.

Genesis 22:3-4

The two men stayed with the donkey. Abraham and Isaac walked up the mountain. Abraham took a knife. Isaac took some wood.

Genesis 22:5-6

Isaac asked where the lamb was for the sacrifice. Abraham told him not to worry.

Genesis 22:7-8

Abraham built an altar. He put wood on it.

Genesis 22:9

Abraham tied Isaac and put him on the altar. He held the knife over Isaac. Abraham was ready to sacrifice his son. But an angel spoke to Abraham. He told Abraham not to sacrifice Isaac. Abraham had obeyed God. God loved Abraham.

Genesis 22:9-12

Abraham looked around. He saw a ram in the bushes. God had given the ram for the sacrifice. Abraham sacrificed the ram on the altar.

Genesis 22:13

God was happy Abraham had obeyed him. God said he would bless Abraham's family.

Genesis 22:16-18

Abraham and Isaac went home. Abraham had obeyed God. He was willing to let his son die.

Genesis 22:16, 19

What Abraham did was like what Heavenly Father did. Heavenly Father was willing to let his son, Jesus Christ, die for us. Heavenly Father and Abraham loved their sons. Jesus and Isaac loved their fathers and obeyed them.

Jacob 4:5

JACOB AND ESAU

CHAPTER 10

Isaac grew to be a man. He married Rebekah. They wanted to have a baby. They asked God to let them have a baby.

Genesis 25:20-21

God answered their prayers. Rebekah had twin boys. The boys were named Esau and Jacob. Esau was born first.

Genesis 25:22-26

In those days the father gave the first son a blessing. It was called the birthright blessing. Esau should get this blessing when he grew up.

Genesis 25:25, 31

Esau liked to hunt. Jacob stayed at home.

Genesis 25:27

One day Esau came home very hungry. Jacob had made some pottage. (Pottage is like soup.)

Genesis 25:29

Esau asked Jacob for some pottage. Jacob said he could have some. But Esau must give him something. He must let Jacob have the birthright blessing.

Genesis 25:30-31

43

Esau was very hungry. He did not care about the blessing. He said Jacob could have it. Jacob gave him the pottage.

Genesis 25:32-34

Isaac became old. He gave Jacob a blessing. It was the birthright blessing. Isaac said Jacob would be a great man. He would be the leader of Esau and many other people.

Genesis 27:1-29

Esau was sad because he did not have the birthright blessing. Esau was angry at Jacob. He hated Jacob.

Genesis 27:34, 41

JACOB AND HIS FAMILY

CHAPTER 11

Isaac talked to Jacob. He said Jacob should not marry any of the girls from Canaan. Jacob should go to another land. There Jacob would find a girl to marry.

Genesis 28:1-2

Jacob started on his way.

Genesis 28:5

One night Jesus Christ came to him. Jesus said Jacob would have many children. Jacob's family would have all of the land of Canaan. Canaan was the promised land.

Genesis 28:12-15

Jacob promised to obey God. He promised to pay tithing.

Genesis 28:20-22

One day Jacob stopped by a well. He saw many sheep. He met a girl named Rachel. He helped her give her sheep water.

Genesis 29:1-2, 10

Jacob met Rachel's father. His name was Laban. He was glad to see Jacob. Jacob said he wanted to marry Rachel. Laban said Jacob could marry Rachel. But Jacob must work for him.

Genesis 29:13-14, 18-20

Jacob worked for Laban for seven years. He worked very hard. Laban gave him Leah for his wife. Leah was Rachel's sister.

Genesis 29:20-25

Laban let Jacob marry Rachel, too. But Jacob had to work for seven more years.

Genesis 29:26-28

Jacob had many children. He became rich. He had many animals.

Genesis 30:1-24, 43

Jacob worked for Laban for many years. Then Jesus told Jacob to go back to his own land. So he took his family and animals and left Laban's house. They went to the promised land.

Genesis 31:3, 17-18, 41

On the way Jesus Christ came to Jacob. Jacob asked Jesus for a blessing. Jesus blessed Jacob.

Jesus said Jacob would have a new name. His name would be Israel. Israel would have the priesthood.

Genesis 32:24-30

On his way home Jacob met Esau. Jacob thought Esau still hated him. Jacob bowed down to Esau.

Genesis 33:1-3

But Esau did not hate Jacob any more. He and Jacob hugged each other. They loved each other.

Genesis 33:4-15

Jacob and his family went on to Canaan. Esau and his family went to another place.

Genesis 33:16-20

Jacob had 12 sons. They were called the 12 sons of Israel. Each son and his family was called a tribe. Israel's family became the 12 tribes of Israel. They were called Israelites.

Genesis 35:22; 49:1-28; Exodus 9:7

JOSEPH

CHAPTER 12

Jacob's family lived in the land of Canaan. It was the promised land.

Genesis 37:1

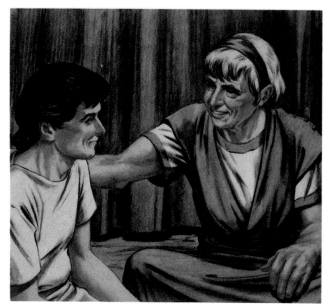

Joseph was one of Jacob's sons. He was 17 years old.

Genesis 37:2

Jacob loved Joseph more than he loved his other sons. This made the other sons angry. Jacob made a beautiful coat for Joseph. It had many colors.

Genesis 37:3-4

Joseph had two dreams. He told his dreams to his brothers. His dreams meant that he would be their leader.

Genesis 37:5-10

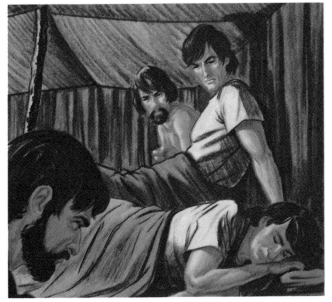

Joseph's brothers did not want him to be their leader. They hated him.

Genesis 37:8, 11

Joseph's brothers took care of the animals. They took the animals far from home to find food.

Genesis 37:12

One day Jacob told Joseph to go find his brothers. Jacob wanted to know if they were all right.

Genesis 37:13-14

Joseph went to look for his brothers. They saw him coming. They wanted to kill Joseph.

Genesis 37:18-20

One brother did not want to kill Joseph. He said they should put Joseph into a hole in the ground.

They took Joseph's coat away from him. They put Joseph in the hole.

Genesis 37:21-24

Some men came along riding on camels. Joseph's brothers took him out of the hole. They sold him to the men. The men took Joseph to Egypt.

Genesis 37:25-28

The brothers killed a goat. They put the goat's blood on Joseph's coat. They took the coat to their father.

Genesis 37:31-32

Jacob saw the blood on Joseph's coat. He thought a wild animal had killed Joseph.

Genesis 37:33

Jacob cried. He was sad for a long time. He loved Joseph very much. He thought Joseph was dead.

Genesis 37:34-35

JOSEPH IN EGYPT

CHAPTER 13

The men who bought Joseph took him to Egypt. They sold him to a man named Potiphar.

Genesis 37:36

Potiphar was a soldier for the king of Egypt. Potiphar made Joseph his slave. God helped Joseph to do good work.

Genesis 39:1-3

Potiphar saw that God helped Joseph. Potiphar liked and trusted Joseph. He made Joseph the leader of all his servants. Joseph took care of everything Potiphar had.

Genesis 39:3-6

Potiphar's wife also liked Joseph. She tried to make Joseph kiss her. Joseph knew this was not right.

Genesis 39:7-9

Joseph ran away from her.

Genesis 39:11-12

Potiphar's wife was angry. She told Potiphar lies about Joseph. She said Joseph tried to kiss her. Potiphar believed his wife.

Genesis 39:16-20

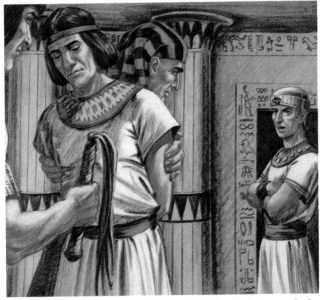

Potiphar was angry at Joseph. He put Joseph in prison.

Genesis 39:19-20

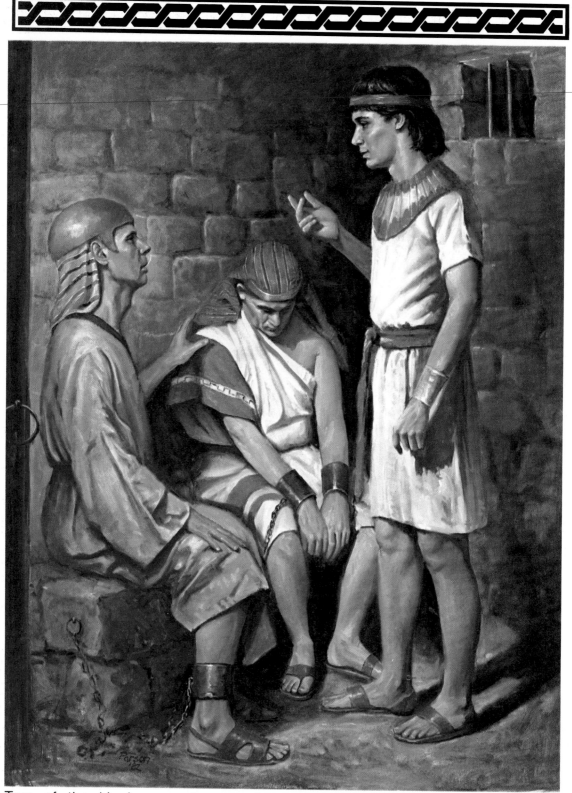

Two of the king's servants were in prison with Joseph. They told Joseph about their dreams. Joseph told them what their dreams meant. One servant was killed. The other was let out of prison. Joseph stayed in prison for two years.

Genesis 40; 41:1

The king of Egypt had some dreams. He did not understand his dreams. No one could tell him what they meant. The king's servant remembered Joseph. He told the king about Joseph. He said Joseph would understand the king's dreams.

Genesis 41:1-13

The king sent for Joseph. Joseph said God told him what the king's dreams meant. Joseph said the people in Egypt would have more food than they needed for seven years. Then there would be a famine. No food would grow for seven years. Joseph said the people must store food. Then they would have food when the famine came.

Genesis 41:14-36

The king believed Joseph. He made Joseph a leader of the people. The people did what Joseph told them to do. They stored food for seven years.

Genesis 41:37-49

After seven years there was a famine. No food grew. People went to Joseph to buy food. Then the people had enough to eat. They were glad they obeyed Joseph.

Genesis 41:54-57

JOSEPH'S BROTHERS IN EGYPT

CHAPTER 14

The famine was in other lands, too. People heard about the food in Egypt. They went to Egypt to buy food. Jacob sent his oldest sons to Egypt to buy food.

Genesis 41:57; 42:1-4

Joseph saw his brothers. They did not know him. He did not tell them he was their brother. Joseph told them to bring all the brothers to Egypt. They bought some food and went home.

Genesis 42:7 Genesis 42:19-20

When the food was gone, the brothers went back to Egypt. Joseph took them to his house.

Genesis 43:15-16

Joseph told his brothers who he was. They were afraid because they had sold him. Genesis 45:3

Joseph said they should not be afraid. God sent him to Egypt to save them from the famine. He told them to tell his father he was alive. Joseph said all of Jacob's family should come to Egypt. He would take care of them. Genesis 45:4-13

The brothers were happy. They went home. They told Jacob that Joseph was alive. Jacob was very happy. Genesis 45:24-28

Jacob and his sons took their families to Egypt. They were called Israelites. The king of Egypt gave the Israelites land and animals. They were happy to be in Egypt. Genesis 46:5-7; 47:5-7

Before Jacob died, he blessed all of his sons.

Genesis 49:1-28

THE BABY MOSES

CHAPTER 15

Joseph and the king of Egypt died. Many years went by. The Israelites lived in Egypt a long time. They had many children. One king of Egypt did not like the Israelites. He thought there were too many of them. He was afraid they would take his land away from him.

Exodus 1:6-10

The king made the Israelites slaves. The Egyptians made them work hard and were mean to them.

Exodus 1:11-14

The king said all the Israelite baby boys must be killed. He sent people to kill them.

Exodus 1:22

One Israelite mother was afraid they would find her baby boy. She hid him for three months. Then the mother put her baby in a basket. She put the basket in the tall grass by the river. The baby's sister, Miriam, stood by to watch the baby.

Exodus 2:1-4

The king of Egypt had a daughter. She went to the river. She saw the basket and opened it. The baby began to cry. The king's daughter was sorry for the baby. She wanted to take him to her home. She needed someone to take care of the baby. She wanted to be his mother.

Exodus 2:5-10

Miriam went to the king's daughter. Miriam said she would find an Israelite woman to take care of the baby. She ran and got her mother. Her mother came to take care of the baby.

Exodus 2:7-9

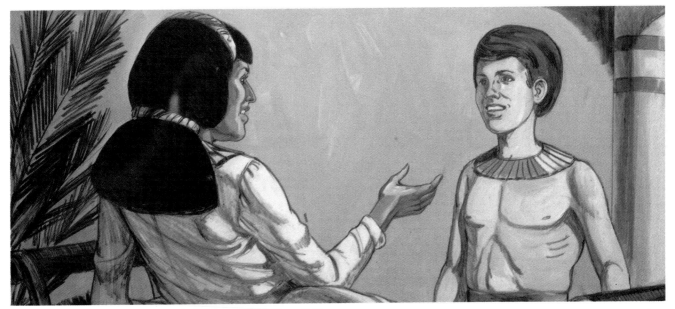

They took the baby to the king's house. The king's daughter named him Moses. Moses grew up in the king's house.

Exodus 2:10-11

THE PROPHET MOSES

CHAPTER 16

Moses grew to be a man. His people, the Israelites, were slaves in Egypt. He saw his people working too hard. Moses was sad for them.

Exodus 2:11

One day Moses saw an Egyptian beating an Israelite. He was angry. He killed the Egyptian.

Exodus 2:11-12

The king of Egypt heard that Moses had killed the Egyptian. He said he would have Moses killed. Moses was afraid. He left Egypt and went to another land. He stayed there for many years.

Exodus 2:15-23

One day Moses went upon a mountain. He saw a bush that was on fire. The bush did not burn up. It was a miracle. It showed Moses the power of God. Moses went close to it. Jesus Christ spoke to Moses from the bush. Jesus knew that the Israelites were not happy. He did not want them to be slaves. So he told Moses to lead the Israelites out of Egypt to the promised land. But Moses thought he could not lead the Israelites. Jesus said Aaron could help Moses. Aaron was Moses' brother.

Exodus 3:2-4, 10-22; 4:10-17; 3 Nephi 15:4-5

Moses was a prophet of God. Moses and Aaron went to the king of Egypt. They asked him to let the Israelites leave Egypt. The king said he would not let them go.

Exodus 5:1-9

Jesus said he would help Moses and Aaron. Jesus would show the king of Egypt his power. Then the king would let the Israelites go.

Exodus 6:1-6

Moses told the king Jesus would change the water in the rivers to blood. Jesus did change the water in Egypt to blood. The people could not drink the water. The fish died.

Exodus 7:14-21

Again Moses asked the king to let the Israelites go. But the king would not let them go.

Exodus 7:22-25

Jesus sent many frogs to Egypt. The frogs were everywhere. They were in the homes and the beds of the people. The king said he would let the Israelites go if the frogs went away. Jesus made the frogs die. But the king had lied to Moses. He would not let the Israelites go.

Exodus 8:1-15

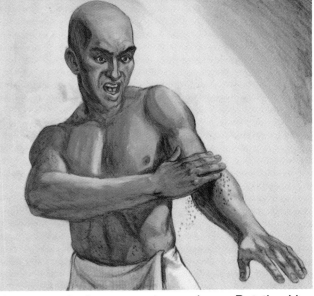

Jesus made lice come everywhere. But the king still would not let the Israelites go.

Exodus 8:16-19

Jesus made flies come everywhere to the Egyptians. The king told Moses that he would let the Israelites go if the flies went away. The flies went away. But the king had lied again. He would not let them go.

Exodus 8:22-32

Moses said that Jesus would make the Egyptians' animals die. Soon their animals died. But the king still would not let the Israelites go.

Exodus 9:1-7

Jesus put bad sores on the Egyptians. Then Jesus sent a bad hail storm. The storm killed everyone who was outside. The king said that he would let the Israelites go. Moses prayed, and the storm stopped. But the king would not let them go.

Exodus 9:8-35

Jesus sent grasshoppers to eat all the food. The grasshoppers ate all the fruit and green plants. Still the king would not let the Israelites go.

Exodus 10:4-20

Jesus sent darkness for three days. The Egyptians could not see anything. But the Israelites had light in their houses. The king of Egypt still would not let the Israelites go.

Exodus 10:21-27

Jesus told Moses a sickness would come. The oldest child in every Egyptian family would die. Even the king's oldest son would die.

Exodus 11:1-6, 10

THE PASSOVER

CHAPTER 17

Jesus told Moses how to save the Israelite children. He said each Israelite father should get a lamb. The lamb must have nothing wrong with it.

Exodus 12:3-5

Moses told the Israelites to kill the lambs. They obeyed him. They put the lambs' blood on their doors. The sickness would pass over the houses with blood on their doors. If there were no blood on the door the oldest child would die.

Exodus 12:6-11

The Israelites cooked the lamb meat and ate it. They stayed in their houses.

Exodus 12:28

That night the oldest child of each Egyptian family died. Even the king's oldest son died.

Exodus 12:29-30

The sickness passed over the houses with blood on the door. The Israelite children did not die. Jesus called this the Passover. He told the Israelites to remember the Passover. He said they should have a Passover dinner every year. They should remember that Jesus saved their children.

Exodus 12:14, 41-42

The king was afraid everyone in Egypt would die. He sent for Moses and Aaron. He told them to take the Israelites and leave Egypt.

Exodus 12:30-33

The Israelites left Egypt. Moses led them. Jesus showed Moses where to go.

Exodus 13:20-22

The king of Egypt still wanted the Israelites for slaves. He took his army and chased them.

Exodus 14:5-9

The Israelites came to the Red Sea. They saw the Egyptian army coming. The Israelites were afraid. They thought they would be killed. They would rather be slaves than be killed.

Exodus 14:10-12

Moses told them not to be afraid. He said Jesus would help them.

Exodus 14:10, 13-14

Jesus told Moses to raise his hand over the sea. A strong wind divided the sea. It was a miracle. It showed the Israelites God's power. Jesus stopped the Egyptians. The Israelites walked across on dry ground. Then the Egyptians went after them.

Exodus 14:16, 19, 21-23

The Israelites were safe on the other side. Jesus told Moses to raise his hand over the sea again.

The sea covered the Egyptians. They were killed.

Exodus 14:26-30

Now the Israelites were free. They sang songs and danced and thanked God. They would always remember the Passover. They would always remember that Jesus led them out of Egypt.

Exodus 15:1-22

THE ISRAELITES IN THE WILDERNESS

CHAPTER 18

Moses and the Israelites traveled for three days. They were thirsty. They came to some water. It tasted bad. They could not drink it.

Exodus 15:22-23

Jesus told Moses to put a tree in the water. The tree made the water taste good. The people drank and went on.

Exodus 15:24-27

They traveled many days in the wilderness. Their food was gone. They were hungry. They were angry at Moses. Jesus gave them something to eat. They called it manna. It tasted like bread and honey. The manna was on the ground each morning.

Exodus 16:1-15, 31

Jesus told them to pick up only as much manna as they needed each day. Some people did not obey. They picked up too much. They kept some for the next day. But the next morning the manna was full of worms. It smelled bad. They could not eat it.

Exodus 16:16-21

Jesus said they should not pick up manna on the sabbath. They should pick up a lot of manna the day before. Then they would not have to work on the sabbath. They could keep the Sabbath day holy. The manna stayed good on the Sabbath.

Exodus 16:22-26

The Israelites traveled on in the wilderness. Again there was no water to drink. They were angry at Moses. Moses prayed.

Exodus 17:1-4

Jesus told Moses to hit a rock. Moses obeyed Jesus. He hit the rock and water came out. It was a miracle. It showed the people God's power. The Israelites drank the water and traveled on.

Exodus 17:5-7

74

THE TEN COMMANDMENTS

CHAPTER 19

The Israelites traveled in the wilderness for two months. They came to Mount Sinai.

Exodus 19:1

Moses went up the mountain. Jesus Christ spoke to him. Jesus told Moses to tell the Israelites how they had been blessed. Jesus had led them out of Egypt. He said the people should obey his commandments. He would bless them.

Exodus 19:3-6; 3 Nephi 15:5

Moses went down the mountain. He told the people what Jesus said. The people promised to obey. They would do what Jesus said. And Jesus would bless them.

Exodus 19:7-8

Jesus wanted the Israelites to hear his voice. Moses told them to stand at the bottom of a mountain. The mountain was called Mount Sinai.

Exodus 19:1, 9-17

A cloud of smoke came on the mountain. Jesus was in the cloud. The mountain shook. Jesus spoke to the people.

Exodus 19:16-25; 20:22

Jesus Christ told the people the ten commandments. Jesus said:

1. Thou shalt have no other gods before me.
2. Thou shalt not make unto thee any graven image.
3. Thou shalt not take the name of the Lord thy God in vain.
4. Remember the sabbath day, to keep it holy.
5. Honor thy father and thy mother.
6. Thou shalt not kill.
7. Thou shalt not commit adultery.
8. Thou shalt not steal.
9. Thou shalt not bear false witness against thy neighbor.
10. Thou shalt not covet.

Exodus 20:1-17

The people heard Jesus Christ. They were afraid. They did not want Jesus to talk to them. They wanted him to talk to Moses. Then Moses could tell them what Jesus said. Moses went back up Mount Sinai. Jesus gave other commandments for the people.

Exodus 20:18-26; Exodus 21-23

Moses told Aaron and Aaron's two sons to come up the mountain. He also told 70 elders to come up. The men went up the mountain. They saw Jesus.

Exodus 24:1-11

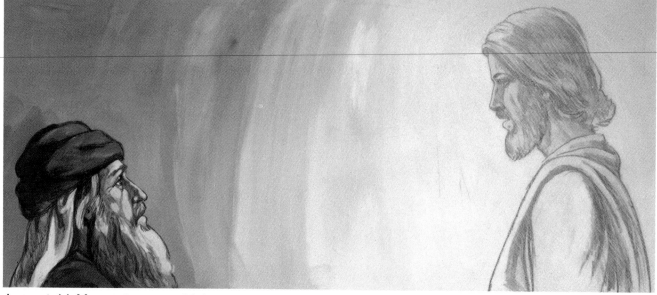

Jesus told Moses to come higher on the mountain. Jesus wrote the commandments on stone with his finger. Jesus gave Moses the commandments.

Exodus 24:12; Exodus 31:18

Moses was gone 40 days and 40 nights. He did not eat or drink all that time.

Exodus 24:18; Exodus 34:28; Deut. 9:9-13, 18

THE GOLDEN CALF

CHAPTER 20

One of the 70 elders on Mount Sinai was Joshua. He waited there for Moses. Aaron and the other men went down the mountain.

Exodus 24:14

Some of the Israelites came to Aaron. They said Moses had been gone a long time. They did not know what he was doing. They were tired of waiting for him. They wanted Aaron to make an idol for them to worship. They did not want to worship God.

Exodus 32:1, 4

All the men and women wore gold earrings. Aaron told them to bring the earrings to him. He made an idol out of the gold. The idol looked like a calf.

Exodus 32:2-4

Aaron built an altar near the golden calf. Some of the Israelites made sacrifices on the altar. They worshiped the golden calf. It was wicked to make sacrifices to the golden calf.

Exodus 32:5-7

Moses was on Mount Sinai with Jesus. Jesus said some of the Israelites were doing wicked things. They had forgotten Jesus. Jesus was angry. He said the wicked Israelites must die. He said Moses would be blessed because he was righteous.

Exodus 32:7-10

Moses asked Jesus to remember his promise to the Israelites. Jesus had promised they would be a large family. They would have the priesthood. They would have the promised land.

Exodus 32:11-13; Abraham 2:9; Genesis 12:1-3

Moses came down from Mount Sinai. Moses had two large stones in his hands. Jesus had written the commandments on the stones with his finger.

Exodus 32:15-16

Moses saw the golden calf. He saw the Israelites dancing. Some had no clothes on. Moses was very angry. He threw the stones down. They broke.

Exodus 32:18-19, 25

Moses threw the golden calf in the fire. He was angry at Aaron. Moses asked Aaron why he had helped the Israelites to be wicked. Aaron said he did what the Israelites wanted him to do.

Exodus 32:20-24

Moses asked the righteous Israelites to come to him. He said they would be blessed. He told them the wicked Israelites must die.

Exodus 32:26-29

Jesus told Moses to bring two new stones to the top of Mount Sinai. Jesus again wrote the Ten Commandments on them. Moses took the commandments down to the people.

Exodus 34:1-4

THE TABERNACLE

Jesus Christ talked to Moses on Mount Sinai. Jesus said the Israelites should build a tabernacle. A tabernacle is a place to learn about God. Jesus would come to the tabernacle.

Jesus showed Moses what the tabernacle should look like. He told Moses how to build it. Jesus told Moses which men should build the tabernacle. Jesus blessed the men so they could do good work.

Exodus 24:16; Exodus 25:1-9; Exodus 35:30-35

The Israelites obeyed Jesus. They gave gold and silver for the tabernacle. They gave animal skins for the roof. The women made beautiful cloth for the walls.

Exodus 35:21-29

The Israelites built the tabernacle the way Jesus told them. The tabernacle was like a tent. It had a wall of curtains. There was a yard inside the wall. An altar for sacrifices was in the yard.

Exodus 36-39

A small building was in the yard. It was also like a tent. It had two rooms. A gold altar was in one room.

Exodus 36-39

A beautiful, big box was in the other room. It was called the ark of the covenant. The stones with the commandments written on them were kept in the ark of the covenant.

Exodus 36-39

Moses was happy because the Israelites obeyed Jesus. Moses blessed the people. He blessed the tabernacle. He blessed Aaron and his sons and gave them the priesthood. Jesus chose other men to help them. Aaron and his sons burned sacrifices for the people. The other men helped take care of the tabernacle.

Exodus 39:32, 42-43; Exodus 40:9-16

The tabernacle was a holy place like a temple. Jesus came there. The people went there to learn about God and to do his work. They made sacrifices there.

D&C 124:38; Exodus 40:34; Leviticus 1

Jesus put a cloud above the tabernacle in the day. He put a fire above the tabernacle at night. The fire and the cloud showed the Israelites that Jesus was there.

Exodus 40:34, 38

When the cloud moved, the Israelites took down the tabernacle. They carried it with them in the wilderness. They followed the cloud.

Exodus 40:36-37

40 YEARS IN THE WILDERNESS

CHAPTER 22

The Israelites lived at Mount Sinai for a year. Then the cloud went away from the tabernacle. The Israelites followed the cloud into the wilderness. The priests carried the ark of the covenant in front of them. Jesus said he would lead the Israelites to the promised land.

Numbers 10:11-12, 33-34; Exodus 3:17

The Israelites followed Moses. They did not like the wilderness. They were not happy. They were sorry they had left Egypt.

Numbers 10:13; 11:1-5

Jesus sent them manna. The people got tired of eating manna. They wanted some meat. Jesus sent some quails for them.

Numbers 11:4-9, 18, 31-33

The Israelites came to the land of Canaan. It was the promised land. Moses sent 12 spies into the land of Canaan.

Numbers 13:2-3

The spies came back. They brought many kinds of fruit. They said the land was very good. But some of the spies were afraid of the people of Canaan. The people were big and strong. They lived in big cities with walls around them.

Numbers 13:21-31

The Israelites listened to the spies. The Israelites were afraid. They thought they could not capture the land of Canaan. They were angry at Moses. They wanted to go back to Egypt. They did not have faith in God.

Numbers 14:1-4

Jesus was angry at the Israelites. He told Moses he would not help them any more. Moses asked God to forgive them. Jesus forgave them. But he would not let them go into the promised land. He told Moses to take the Israelites back into the wilderness.

Numbers 14:11-25

God said they must live in the wilderness for 40 years. The older Israelites did not have faith in God. They would die in the wilderness. Their children would grow up and go into the promised land. The Israelites went back into the wilderness.

Numbers 14:23, 29-34; Deuteronomy 2:1

One day the Israelites were very thirsty. There was no water to drink. They told Moses they wanted water.

Numbers 20:2-5

Jesus Christ told Moses how to get water. Moses hit a rock two times with his rod. Water came out of the rock. The people drank the water.

Numbers 20:6-11

Moses led the people in the wilderness for 40 years. He taught them the commandments of God.

Numbers 14:33-34; Deuteronomy

When Moses was 120 years old, God told him to go to a mountain. Moses saw the land of Canaan. It was the land God had promised the Israelites. Then God took Moses.

Deuteronomy 32:49-52; 34:1-7; Alma 45:19

JOSHUA

CHAPTER 23

Jesus chose Joshua to be the prophet after Moses. Jesus told Joshua to lead the Israelites into the promised land. Other people were living there. Jesus would help the Israelites get the land.

Joshua 1:1-9

Joshua sent spies across the river into the promised land. The spies came back. They told Joshua the people in the land were afraid of the Israelites. The Israelites came to the Jordan River.

Joshua 3:1; 2:1-24

The Israelites were ready to cross the Jordan River. The priests carried the ark of the covenant into the river. The water stopped. The Israelites crossed the river on dry ground. Jesus was helping Joshua the way that he had helped Moses.

Joshua 3:14-17

Then the priests carried the ark of the covenant to the other side. The water started again.

Joshua 4:17-18

Joshua led the Israelites to the city of Jericho. Jericho had high walls around it. The people of Jericho closed the city gates to keep the Israelites out. The people in Jericho thought they were safe.

Joshua 5:13; 6:1

Jesus sent an angel to Joshua. The angel told Joshua how to capture Jericho. Joshua obeyed the angel.

Joshua 5:13-15; 6:1-5

Joshua told some priests to carry the ark of the covenant in front of the army. The army marched around the walls of Jericho once a day for six days.

Joshua 6:6-14

Seven priests blew their horns. The other men did not make any noise.

Joshua 6:10, 13

On the seventh day the army marched around Jericho seven times. Then Joshua told all the men to shout. They shouted. The walls of Jericho fell down. They captured Jericho. Jesus had helped the Israelites.

Joshua 6:15-16, 20

All the people heard that the Israelites had captured Jericho. They were afraid. They knew Jesus was helping Joshua and the Israelites. Joshua led the people from city to city. They captured all the promised land.

Joshua 6:27; 11:23

This was the land God promised to Abraham, Isaac and Jacob. God had told Joseph, Moses, and Joshua that this land would be the land of Israel. God kept his promise.

Genesis 50:24; Deuteronomy 34:4; Joshua 1:2

Joshua built an altar to burn sacrifices. All the people met together. Joshua read the commandments Jesus gave Moses.

Joshua 8:30-35

Then Joshua divided the land into 12 parts. He gave one part of the land to each tribe of Israel. The people built new homes and cities and farms.

Joshua 11:23

Joshua became old. He called the leaders of Israel together. He told them God had given them the land. God had helped them win their battles. They could keep the land if they were righteous. They would lose the land if they were wicked.

Joshua 23

Joshua was a great prophet of God. He spoke to all the Israelites. He told them God had blessed them. He told them to obey God. Joshua told them to choose whom they would obey. He said he and his family would obey God. The people went back to their homes. Then Joshua died.

Joshua 24:1-29

RUTH AND NAOMI

CHAPTER 24

After many years there was a famine. It did not rain for a long time. Food would not grow. The people became very hungry.

Ruth 1:1

A woman named Naomi lived in Bethlehem. She and her husband took their family to a land called Moab to find food.

Ruth 1:1-2

Naomi's husband died there. Naomi and her two sons stayed in Moab.

Ruth 1:3-4

Her sons married women from Moab. Their names were Ruth and Orpah.

Ruth 1:4

They lived in Moab for ten years. Naomi's sons died there.

Ruth 1:4-5

Naomi wanted to go back to Bethlehem. She told Ruth and Orpah to go home to their own families.

Ruth 1:6-13

Orpah went to her family. Ruth wanted to go to Bethlehem with Naomi. She loved Naomi. She wanted to live where Naomi lived. She wanted to be with Naomi always.

Ruth 1:14-17

Ruth and Naomi went back to Bethlehem. Ruth went to the fields to get wheat and barley. She used them to make bread.

Ruth 1:19-22

A righteous man named Boaz lived in Bethlehem. He had many wheat and barley fields.

Ruth 2:1

Boaz saw Ruth working to get food for Naomi. He was kind to Ruth. He told her to come to his fields always. He said God would bless Ruth for being kind to Naomi.

Ruth 2:5-8

Boaz married Ruth. Naomi was happy for her.

Ruth 4:13

Ruth and Boaz had a son. Naomi helped Ruth take care of the baby. The baby's name was Obed.

Ruth 4:13, 16-17

Obed grew up and had children. His grandson was King David.

Ruth 4:21-22

Many years later Jesus would be born into this family.

Matthew 1:1-17

SAMUEL

CHAPTER 25

After Joshua died, God chose new leaders for the Israelites. They were called judges. Eli was one of the judges. He was also God's priest. He took care of the tabernacle. He burned sacrifices for the people.

1 Samuel 1:3, 9

One day a woman named Hannah came to the tabernacle to pray. She was sad because she had no children.

1 Samuel 1:4-6

Hannah asked God to let her have a baby boy. She promised to teach the baby to obey God. She would take him to the tabernacle to serve God.

1 Samuel 1:10-11

Eli heard Hannah pray. He told her God would give her a baby boy. Hannah was happy.

1 Samuel 1:12-18

God blessed her. She had a baby boy. She named him Samuel. Hannah took good care of Samuel.

1 Samuel 1:19-23

One day Hannah took Samuel to Eli. She asked Eli to teach Samuel to do God's work. Hannah left Samuel with Eli and went home. Samuel helped Eli do God's work.

1 Samuel 1:24-2:11

Samuel learned to help others. God was happy with him. The people who came to the tabernacle liked Samuel.

1 Samuel 2:18, 21, 26; 3:1

Eli had two sons. They helped him at the tabernacle. But they did not help the people. They did many wicked things. The people told Eli his sons were wicked. But Eli still let his sons work in the tabernacle.

1 Samuel 2:12-17, 22-23

One day God sent a prophet to Eli. The prophet told Eli God was not happy with his sons. They had the priesthood, but they were not righteous. They could not keep the priesthood. God would give the priesthood to a righteous man. The prophet said Eli's sons would be killed. Eli was very sad.

1 Samuel 2:27-36

One night Eli was in bed. Samuel was in bed in another room. Samuel heard someone call his name.

1 Samuel 3:2-4

Samuel thought Eli had called him. He ran to Eli. Eli said he had not called Samuel. He told Samuel to lie down again, and Samuel did.

1 Samuel 3:5

Samuel heard someone call his name three times. Each time he went to Eli. And each time Eli told Samuel to go back to bed.

1 Samuel 3:6-8

At last Eli told Samuel that God was calling him. Eli told Samuel to go to his room and to listen to God.

1 Samuel 3:9

God told Samuel Eli had let his sons be wicked. So Eli and his sons could not work in the tabernacle. They would die.

1 Samuel 3:10-14; 2:34

In the morning Samuel told Eli what God said. Eli knew that God had spoken to Samuel.

1 Samuel 3:18

Later Eli's sons were killed in a battle. Eli died when he heard about his sons.

1 Samuel 4:17-18

Samuel grew up, and God blessed him. God chose Samuel to be the new prophet and judge. Samuel had the priesthood. God came to Samuel and spoke to him. All the people knew Samuel was a prophet of God.

1 Samuel 3:19-21; 7:15-17

KING SAUL

CHAPTER 26

Samuel was the judge and prophet of Israel. He went to every city to judge the people. When Samuel became old, he chose his sons to be judges. They were not good judges.

1 Samuel 7:15-17; 8:1-3

The elders of Israel came to Samuel. They said the people did not want judges. They wanted a king.

1 Samuel 8:4-5

Samuel prayed to God. God told him to do what the people wanted. God knew they wanted a king. They did not want God to lead them. God told Samuel to tell them the wicked things that a king would do.

1 Samuel 8:6-9

Samuel obeyed God. He told the people God would let them have a king. But kings would take their fields and animals. They would take their children for servants. Some day they would not want a king.

1 Samuel 18:10-18

One day God talked to Samuel. He said a young man would come the next day. This man would be the king.

1 Samuel 9:15-16

The next day a young man came to Samuel. He was a righteous Israelite. He was big and strong. His name was Saul.

1 Samuel 9:1-2, 17-19

Samuel asked Saul to stay with him. Samuel anointed Saul with oil. Saul was to be the king of Israel.

1 Samuel 9:19; 10:1

Samuel called all the Israelites together. He told them God had chosen Saul to be their king. But some of the people did not want Saul to be their king.

1 Samuel 10:17-24, 27

One day some wicked men came to fight the Israelites. Saul called all the men of Israel to fight. He led them.

1 Samuel 11:1-7

Saul was a great leader. The Israelites won the battle. Then all the people were glad Saul was their king. God blessed Saul. He was a king for many years. At first Saul was a good king.

1 Samuel 11:12-15

Then one day Saul was waiting for Samuel. Samuel was coming to burn sacrifices. Samuel was the only man who should burn sacrifices to God. But he was late. Saul did not wait for him. Saul burned the sacrifices. It was wrong for Saul to do that.

1 Samuel 13:8-9

At last Samuel came. He was angry at Saul. Saul had not obeyed God. Samuel told him God would choose another king. Saul was sad.

1 Samuel 13:10-14; 15:11-26

YOUNG DAVID

CHAPTER 27

God told Samuel to go to Bethlehem. A man named Jesse lived there. One of Jesse's sons would be the next king of Israel.

1 Samuel 16:1

Samuel obeyed God. He went to Bethlehem. He took a calf to sacrifice to God.

1 Samuel 16:2-5

Samuel told Jesse and his sons to come to the sacrifice. One of the sons was tall and strong. Samuel thought this son would be the king.

1 Samuel 16:5-6

But God said he had not chosen that son.

1 Samuel 16:7

Jesse's other sons came to Samuel. God had not chosen any of them to be king. Samuel asked if Jesse had any more sons.

1 Samuel 16:8-11

Jesse said his youngest son was not there. His name was David. Samuel told Jesse to send for David.

1 Samuel 16:11

David was taking care of the sheep.

1 Samuel 16:11

David came to Samuel. David was a good boy. God said he had chosen David to be king.

1 Samuel 16:12

Samuel anointed David. He put oil on David's head and blessed him.

1 Samuel 16:12, 13

David was filled with the Holy Ghost. David was anointed to become the next king. Someday he would be the king of Israel.

1 Samuel 16:13

DAVID
AND GOLIATH

CHAPTER 28

There was a war in the land of Israel. King Saul and the Israelites were fighting the Philistines. One of the Philistines was a giant. His name was Goliath. He was very big and strong. The Israelites were afraid of him.

1 Samuel 17:1-7

Goliath shouted to the Israelites. He told them to choose a man to fight him. No one wanted to fight the giant. Goliath shouted to them every morning and every night for 40 days. None of the Israelites would fight him.

1 Samuel 17:4-11, 16

David's brothers were in the Israelite army. Jesse sent David to take some food to them.

1 Samuel 17:13-20.

David saw the giant. He heard Goliath shouting. He saw that the men were afraid of Goliath.

1 Samuel 17:23-24

David said he would fight the giant. His brothers were angry. They said David should be taking care of the sheep.

1 Samuel 17:26-37

David knew God would help him. He picked up five stones. He took his sling and went to fight Goliath.

1 Samuel 17:37, 40

Goliath saw that David was young. He was angry. He shouted at David and made fun of him. David shouted back. He said God would help him kill Goliath.

1 Samuel 17:41-47

Goliath came at David to fight. Then David put a stone in his sling and threw the stone.

1 Samuel 17:49

The stone hit Goliath in the head. Goliath fell to the ground.

1 Samuel 17:49

David took Goliath's sword and cut off his head.

1 Samuel 17:50-51

The Philistines saw David kill Goliath. They were afraid and ran away. God had helped David kill the giant.

1 Samuel 17:51-53

KING DAVID

CHAPTER 29

King Saul saw David kill Goliath. He sent for David. Saul told David to come and live in his house. Saul made David a leader of his army.

1 Samuel 17:55-57; 18:2, 5

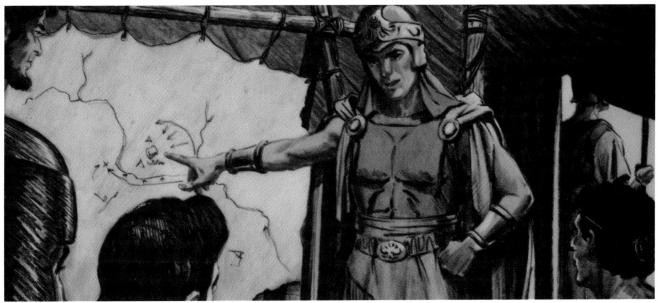

God blessed David. His army won many battles for King Saul. The people of Israel loved David.

1 Samuel 18:6-7

The Israelites and the Philistines were fighting. King Saul and his sons were in the battle. Saul and three of his sons were killed.

1 Samuel 31:1-6

David heard that King Saul was dead. David was sad. He fasted and prayed.

2 Samuel 1:4, 11-12

David became the king of Israel. David was a good king. He loved God and obeyed his commandments.

2 Samuel 5:1-5, 10-12

One evening David saw a beautiful woman. Her name was Bath-sheba. She was married to a man named Uriah.

2 Samuel 11:2-3

Uriah was a soldier. He was fighting in the war. David wanted Uriah to die. Then David could marry Bath-sheba. It was wicked for David to want Uriah's wife.

2 Samuel 11:6-14

David sent Uriah to the front of the battle. He knew Uriah would be killed. Uriah was killed. It was wicked for David to have Uriah killed.

2 Samuel 11:14-17

David married Bath-sheba. They had a son named Solomon.

2 Samuel 11:27, 12:24

God sent a prophet named Nathan to talk to David. Nathan told David God knew what David had done. God would punish David.

2 Samuel 12:1-15

David knew he had been wicked. He was sorry for his sins. He made sacrifices. He prayed to God to forgive him.

2 Samuel 12:13-20

David suffered because of his sins. He prayed to God often. He tried to be righteous. He was a good king.

2 Samuel 12

David was king for a long time. He became old. He wanted his son Solomon to be the next king. David asked Nathan, the prophet, to anoint Solomon to be king. David told Solomon to obey God's commandments.

1 Kings 1:1, 30-35; 2:1-3, 11

David died and was buried near Jerusalem.

1 Kings 2:10

KING SOLOMON

CHAPTER 30

Solomon became the king of Israel. He loved God.

1 Kings 2:12, 3:3

He asked God to help him be a good king. God was happy Solomon wanted to be righteous. God wanted to bless Solomon. God asked Solomon what blessing he would like. Solomon wanted to be wise. God was glad Solomon chose to be wise. He told Solomon to obey his commandments. Then Solomon would be wise.

1 Kings 3:6-15

Solomon became the wisest man on earth. People came from other lands to ask him questions. He gave them wise answers. Kings and queens came to see him. They brought him beautiful gifts.

1 Kings 4:21, 29-34

The Israelites came to King Solomon when they needed help. One day two women came to him with a baby boy. The women said they lived in the same house. They each had a baby, but one of the babies died. Now both women wanted the baby that was alive. Each mother said he was her baby. They wanted King Solomon to tell them who could keep the baby.

1 Kings 3:16-22

Solomon wanted to find out which woman was the baby's mother. He had a wise plan. He asked for a sword. He told a servant to cut the baby in half. He would give half of the baby to each woman. Solomon would not really let the baby be cut in half. He wanted to see what the women would do. He knew the baby's mother would not let her son be hurt.

1 Kings 3:22-25

One mother told Solomon not to cut the baby in half. She did not want the baby to be hurt. She loved the baby. She said the other woman could have him. The other woman told Solomon to cut the baby in half.

1 Kings 3:26

Then Solomon knew who should keep the baby. The real mother did not want the baby to be hurt. Solomon gave the baby to her. Soon all the Israelites heard what had happened. They knew God had made Solomon wise.

1 Kings 3:27-28

THE TEMPLE

CHAPTER 31

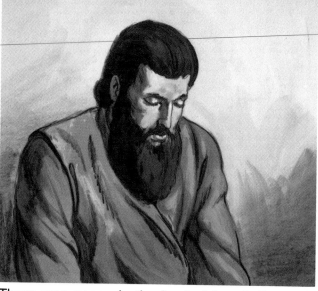

There was peace in the land of Israel. God said King Solomon should build a temple in Jerusalem. It would be the house of God. The ark of the covenant would be in the temple. The people would not need the tabernacle any more because they would have the temple.

1 Kings 5:3-5; 1 Chronicles 28:2-3, 6, 10

Thousands of people helped build the temple. It was made of stone and wood. Men brought the best wood from far away. They cut large stones for the walls of the temple.

1 Kings 5:8-18

The temple was beautiful. It had many rooms. The walls and floors were covered with gold. There were curtains made of beautiful cloth. Gold candlesticks lighted the rooms. There was a golden altar in one room.

1 Kings 6; 2 Chronicles 4

Another room had a pool filled with water. The pool was on the backs of 12 oxen. The oxen were made of brass.

1 Kings 7:23-26; 2 Chronicles 4:2-5

It took seven years to build the temple. At last it was finished. Then Solomon put beautiful gold and silver bowls in the temple.

1 Kings 6:38; 7:51; 2 Chronicles 5:1

The priests brought the ark of the covenant from the tabernacle. They put the ark in the temple. The two stones with the commandments written on them were in the ark.

1 Kings 8:3-9

The priests of Israel came to the temple. They sang songs and thanked God for the temple. The cloud that had been over the tabernacle filled the temple. The temple was the house of God.

1 Kings 8:10-11; 2 Chronicles 5:11-14

Solomon spoke to the Israelites. He told them to obey God's commandments. Then Solomon prayed to God. He asked God to forgive the people when they had repented.

1 Kings 8:12, 22, 33-34

Solomon made sacrifices to God. Fire from heaven came down to the altar. The fire burned the sacrifices.

1 Kings 8:62-63; 2 Chronicles 7:1-3

The people worshiped God. They thanked him for the temple.

2 Chronicles 7:3

God spoke to Solomon. He said Solomon and the Israelites should be righteous. Then he would bless them forever.

1 Kings 9:2-5

124

THE DIVIDED KINGDOM

CHAPTER 32

Solomon was the king of Israel for a long time. He obeyed God for many years.

1 Kings 11:41-42

Solomon had many wives. Some of his wives did not believe in God. They worshiped idols.

1 Kings 11:1-3

When Solomon was old, he forgot God. His wives wanted him to worship their idols. Solomon did the wrong thing. He made sacrifices to the idols. God was angry at him.

1 Kings 11:4-9

God said Solomon's kingdom would be divided after he died. Solomon died. He was buried near his father, David.

1 Kings 11:10-13, 43

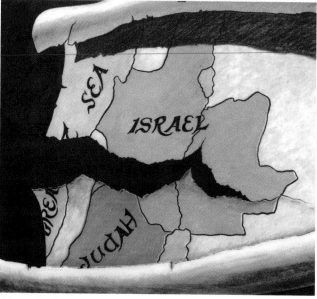

After Solomon died, the 12 tribes of Israel were divided. The south part of the land was called the Kingdom of Judah. Two Israelite tribes lived there. They were called Jews. Rehoboam was the king.

1 Kings 12:1-17

Rehoboam was Solomon's son. He was not a good king. He was mean to the people.

1 Kings 12:14

The north part of the land was called the Kingdom of Israel. Ten Israelite tribes lived there. Jeroboam was their king. Jeroboam was strong and brave, but he was not a good king.

1 Kings 12

Jeroboam made golden idols and burned sacrifices to them. He told the people to worship the idols.

1 Kings 12:27-33

A prophet of God told Jeroboam to repent. But Jeroboam would not repent.

1 Kings 13:1-6, 33-34

Jeroboam and Rehoboam had armies. They fought each other for many years. Jeroboam and Rehoboam were wicked kings. They did not teach the people to obey God.

1 Kings 14:7-10, 16, 21-24; 2 Chronicles 12:13-15

The Israelites became wicked like their kings.

1 Kings 16:2

THE PROPHET ELIJAH

Many years later Ahab became the king of the Kingdom of Israel. He and his people were wicked. They worshiped idols.

1 Kings 16:29-33

Elijah was a prophet of God. Elijah told Ahab and his people to repent. If they did not repent, God would send a famine. There would be no water. The people would have no food.

1 Kings 17:1

King Ahab had a wife named Jezebel. She did not believe in God. She killed the prophets of God. Jezebel wanted to kill Elijah.

1 Kings 16:31; 18:13; 19:1-2

God told Elijah to hide from Jezebel. Elijah hid by a stream of water. He drank from the stream. God sent birds to bring food to Elijah.

1 Kings 17:3-6; 18:4

Then the famine came. There was no water in the stream. Elijah had no water to drink or food to eat.

1 Kings 17:7

God told Elijah to go to a city. He would meet a woman there. The woman would give him food and water.

1 Kings 17:8-9

Elijah met the woman. Her husband was dead. She lived with her son. Elijah asked her for some water and bread. She said she did not have any. She had only a little flour and oil to make bread for her son.

1 Kings 17:10-12

Elijah told her to make some bread for him first. He said God would give her more flour and oil. She would have food until the famine was over. The woman made bread for Elijah.

1 Kings 17:13-15

Elijah ate with the woman and her son. He stayed with the woman and her son for many days. God blessed them. There was always flour and oil to make bread.

1 Kings 17:15-16

One day the woman's son became very sick and died. His mother was sad.

1 Kings 17:17-18

Elijah had the priesthood. He had the power of God. Elijah prayed. He asked God to let the boy live again.

1 Kings 17:19-21

God heard Elijah's prayer. Then a miracle happened. The boy came back to life. Elijah took him to his mother. She knew Elijah was a prophet of God.

1 Kings 17:22-24

ELIJAH AND THE PRIESTS OF BAAL

CHAPTER 34

There were some wicked people in the kingdom of Israel. They worshiped an idol named Baal. There were 850 priests of Baal. They were wicked priests.

1 Kings 18:19

The prophet Elijah talked to King Ahab. He told Ahab to bring all his people to a mountain. Elijah wanted the wicked priests of Baal to come, too.

1 Kings 18:17-19

Elijah said they must choose to worship God or Baal. They could not worship both. It is wicked to worship idols.

1 Kings 18:21

Elijah wanted to show the people that idols have no power. Elijah asked for two bulls for a sacrifice. He asked for some wood. He gave a bull and some of the wood to the priests of Baal. He kept a bull and some wood for his sacrifice.

1 Kings 18:23

Elijah told the priests not to burn the sacrifice. He told the priests to pray to their idol. He said Baal must burn the sacrifice.

1 Kings 18:24-25

The wicked priests prayed to Baal all morning. They jumped on the altar and shouted. Baal did not answer. Baal was only an idol.

1 Kings 18:26

Elijah told the priests to pray louder. He made fun of them. He said their idol must be sleeping.

1 Kings 18:27

The wicked priests prayed louder and louder. They prayed all day. Baal did not answer. The priests' sacrifice did not burn.

1 Kings 18:28-29

Elijah told the people to come close to him. Elijah told them he would pray to God. He said God would send fire down from heaven. God would burn his sacrifice. Elijah built an altar of stones. He dug around the altar. Elijah put the bull and some wood on the altar.

1 Kings 18:30-33

Elijah asked men to bring four barrels of water. He told them to pour the water on the sacrifice. Then he asked the men to bring four more barrels of water. Again they poured the water on the sacrifice. He told them to bring four more barrels of water. They poured the water on the sacrifice, too.

1 Kings 18:33-35

Elijah prayed to God. Elijah wanted the people to worship God. He asked God to help him.

1 Kings 18:36-37

God sent fire down from heaven. The fire burned Elijah's sacrifice. It burned the wood and the stones. It dried up all the water. The people saw the power of God. They knew the idols had no power. All the wicked priests of Baal were killed.

1 Kings 18:38-39 1 Kings 18:40

ELIJAH
TALKS WITH JESUS

CHAPTER 35

King Ahab had a wicked wife named Jezebel. Jezebel heard what Elijah did. She sent a man to Elijah. The man said Jezebel would kill Elijah.

1 Kings 19:1-2

Elijah went into the wilderness so Jezebel could not kill him. He found a place to hide. He slept under a tree.

1 Kings 19:3-5

An angel came to Elijah. The angel gave him food and water. Elijah ate and lay down again. The angel came again. He told Elijah to eat more. The angel said Elijah would travel a long way. Elijah ate and drank again.

1 Kings 19:5-8

Elijah traveled 40 days and 40 nights. He fasted. He did not eat or drink.

1 Kings 19:8

Elijah went to the mountain where Moses had seen the burning bush.

1 Kings 19:8; Exodus 3:1-2

Elijah lived in a cave in the mountain. God asked him what he was doing there. Elijah said the people did not obey God's commandments. They killed God's prophets. Elijah was the only prophet who had not been killed. The people wanted to kill him, too.

1 Kings 19:9-10

God told Elijah to stand on the mountain. A strong wind blew. It was so strong it broke rocks into pieces. After the wind there was an earthquake. Then there was a fire.

1 Kings 19:11-12

After the fire Elijah heard a quiet voice. He knew it was the voice of Jesus Christ. Jesus came to him. He talked to Elijah. Jesus said he would choose a new prophet. His name was Elisha.

1 Kings 19:11, 15-16

ELIJAH AND ELISHA

CHAPTER 36

Elijah was a prophet of God. He had the power of the priesthood. He had the power of God. He had become old. Elisha had followed Elijah for many years.

2 Kings 1:10

God had told Elijah that Elisha would be the next prophet. Elijah and Elisha went to the Jordan River. Elijah hit the water with his coat. The water divided. They walked through on dry land.

1 Kings 19:16; 2 Kings 2:6-8

Elijah and Elisha walked and talked together. Elisha wanted the Holy Ghost to be with him.

2 Kings 2:9-10

Elisha became the prophet. He had the power of the priesthood. He had the power of God. As Elijah went to heaven, he dropped his coat on the ground. Elisha picked it up.

2 Kings 2:11-13

Elisha went back to the Jordan River. He hit the water with Elijah's coat. The water divided. Elisha walked through on dry land. Some righteous Israelites met him. They knew Elisha was the new prophet.

2 Kings 2:13-15

THE PROPHET ELISHA

CHAPTER 37
THREE MIRACLES

Elisha was a prophet. He had faith in God. God helped him do miracles. A miracle shows the power of God.

1 Kings 17:17-24; 2 Kings 2:14-15

The First Miracle

One day a woman came to see Elisha. She was crying. She told Elisha her husband was dead. She had to pay money to a man. If she did not pay the money, he would take her sons away. Elisha wanted to help the woman. He asked what she had in her house. She had a jar with some oil.

2 Kings 4:1-2

Elisha told the woman to get more jars. He told her to pour oil from her jar into them. The woman obeyed Elisha. The oil from her jar filled all the other jars. That was a miracle.

2 Kings 4:3-6

Elisha told the woman to sell the oil and pay the man. Her sons were not taken away. She was happy.

2 Kings 4:7

The Second Miracle

Another woman and her husband asked Elisha to live in their home. They were old and had no children. Elisha told them they would have a son. They did not believe him. But they had a son.

2 Kings 4:8-17

One day the son went to his father's fields. He told his father that his head hurt.

2 Kings 4:18-19

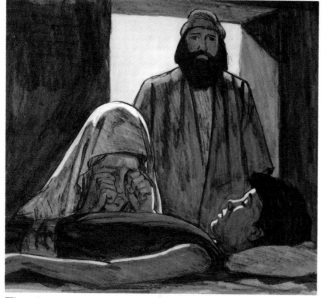

The boy was very sick. His mother held him in her arms. He died. His mother put him on Elisha's bed. Elisha came in and shut the door. He prayed to God and touched the boy.

2 Kings 4:20-34

The boy sneezed seven times and opened his eyes. He was alive again. The mother came into the room. She was happy her son was alive. God helped Elisha bring the boy back to life. That was a miracle.

2 Kings 4:35-37

The Third Miracle

Naaman was a man from another country. He was very sick. He was a leper. He had sores on his body. His skin was falling off.

2 Kings 5:1

Naaman came to Elisha to be healed. Elisha sent his servant to talk to Naaman. He told Naaman to wash seven times in the Jordan River. Then Naaman would be healed.

2 Kings 5:9-10

Naaman was angry because Elisha did not come to heal him. He did not want to do what Elisha said. He started for home. Naaman's servants told him to obey the prophet.

2 Kings 5:11-13

Naaman obeyed Elisha. He washed seven times in the Jordan River. He was healed. His sores were gone. He was not a leper any more. That was a miracle.

2 Kings 5:14

JONAH

CHAPTER 38

Jonah was a prophet of God. God told him to go to a city called Nineveh. The people there were wicked. God told Jonah to tell the people to repent.

Jonah 1:1-2

Jonah did not obey God. Jonah did not want to go to Nineveh. He did not want to tell the people to repent. He got on a ship. The ship was sailing to another city.

Jonah 1:3

God sent a bad storm. The wind blew hard. The men on the ship were afraid it would sink.

Jonah 1:4-5

The captain of the ship went to Jonah. Jonah was sleeping. The captain woke him. He told Jonah to pray and ask God to help them.

Jonah 1:6

The men thought the storm came because Jonah was on the ship. They wanted the storm to stop. They asked Jonah what they should do.

Jonah 1:7-11

Jonah told them to throw him into the water. He knew God sent the storm because of him. He had not obeyed God.

Jonah 1:9-12

The men did not want to throw Jonah into the water. But they knew the storm would stop if they did. So they threw him into the water. The storm stopped.

Jonah 1:13-15

God sent a big fish. The fish swallowed Jonah. Jonah was in the fish for three days and three nights. Jonah prayed to God. He repented. He said he was sorry he had run away. He promised to obey God.

Jonah 1:17; 2:1-9

The fish put Jonah out on dry land. Again God told Jonah to go to Nineveh. He said to tell the people to repent.

Jonah 2:10; 3:1-2

This time Jonah obeyed God. He went to Nineveh. He told the people to repent. If they would not repent, Nineveh would be destroyed.

Jonah 3:3-4

The people did repent. They stopped being wicked. They fasted and prayed. God did not destroy Nineveh.

Jonah 3:5-10

THE ISRAELITES ARE CAPTURED

CHAPTER 39

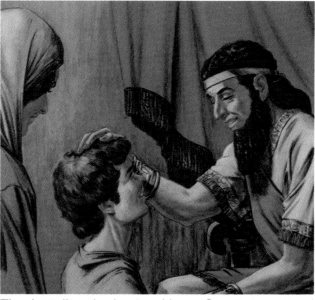

The Israelites had many kings. Some were good kings. They loved God and obeyed his commandments. They helped the Israelites live good lives.

2 Kings 8-24

Most of the kings were wicked. They did not obey God's commandments. They worshiped idols. The people became wicked also.

2 Kings 8-24

There were wars in the land. The ten tribes of Israel were captured. They were taken away as slaves. The Israelites that were left lived in the Kingdom of Judah. They were called Jews.

2 Kings 17:6-23

Lehi and his family lived in Jerusalem 600 years before Christ was born. Many people in Jerusalem were wicked. God sent prophets to teach them. Lehi was one of these prophets.

2 Chronicles 36:14-16; 1 Nephi 1:4

Lehi told the people to repent. He said Jerusalem would be destroyed if they did not repent. But the wicked people did not believe him. Some people laughed at him. Some were angry. They wanted to kill Lehi.

1 Nephi 1:13-20; 2 Chronicles 36:16

God told Lehi to leave Jerusalem with his family. Lehi obeyed God. He and his family traveled to the sea. They built a ship and sailed to America.

1 Nephi 2:2-4; 17:8; 18

Lehi's son Nephi wrote what happened to them. Their story is in the Book of Mormon.

1 Nephi 19:1-4

The Jews heard the prophets, but they did not repent. God sent the king of Babylon and his army to destroy Jerusalem. There was a big battle.

2 Kings 25:1-2

The soldiers from Babylon captured Jerusalem. They took all the gold and silver from the temple. They took beautiful dishes from the temple.

2 Kings 25:13-17

Then they burned the temple of God. They also burned the homes of the people. They broke down the wall around Jerusalem.

2 Kings 25:1-10

Many Jews were killed. Many others were captured. They were taken to Babylon to be slaves.

2 Kings 25:18-21

DANIEL AND
HIS FRIENDS

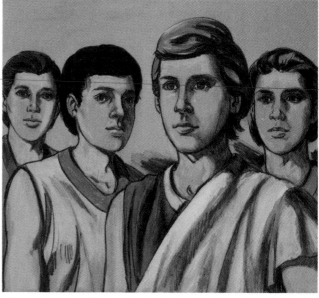

The king of Babylon took the Jews to his land. He took some of their children to live in his house. Four of them were Daniel, Shadrach, Meshach, and Abednego. They learned to speak the king's language.

Daniel 1:1-7

The king sent food and wine to Daniel and his friends. God said they should not eat this food. It was not good for them. They would not eat the food or drink the wine. They asked the king's servants to bring them good food. They asked for water, not wine.

Daniel 1:5-12

The servant gave Daniel and his friends water to drink. He gave them good food for ten days. Daniel and his friends obeyed God. Daniel and his friends looked better than the other children.

Daniel 1:14-16

After three years, Daniel, Shadrach, Meshach, and Abednego were taken to the king. He talked to them. The king said they were wiser than his wise men. God had blessed Daniel and his friends. God had made them strong and wise.

Daniel 1:18-20

The king of Babylon had a dream. When he woke up, he could not remember it. The king asked some of his wise men to tell him what he had dreamed. He also wanted to know what the dream meant.

Daniel 2:1-3

But the wise men could not tell the king his dream. The king was angry. He told his servant to kill all the wise men.

Daniel 2:4-3

But God showed Daniel the king's dream. God told Daniel what it meant. Daniel asked the king's servant not to kill the wise men. Daniel said he could tell the king about the dream.

Daniel 2:19-24

Daniel was taken to the king. He said God told him about the dream. The dream meant the gospel will be taught to all people. Jesus will be the king of all the people on earth. The king of Babylon was happy to know what his dream meant. He made Daniel leader over all the land.

Daniel 2:25-48

SHADRACH, MESHACH, AND ABEDNEGO

The king of Babylon made a gold idol. He told the people to pray to the idol. They would be burned in a furnace if they did not pray to it.

Daniel 3:1-6

Shadrach, Meshach, and Abednego would not pray to the idol. They prayed to God.

Daniel 3:12

Someone told the king. He was angry. He sent for Shadrach, Meshach, and Abednego. The king told them they would be burned in the furnace. Shadrach, Meshach, and Abednego were not afraid. They knew God would save them.

Daniel 3:13-18

The king's servants built a fire in the furnace. They tied Shadrach, Meshach, and Abednego with ropes. The servants threw them into the furnace. The fire was so hot the servants died.

Daniel 3:19-22

The king looked into the furnace. He saw four men walking in the fire. One of the men was an angel of God. God saved Shadrach, Meshach, and Abednego.

Daniel 3:24-25

The king shouted to Shadrach, Meshach, and Abednego. He told them to come out of the furnace. The fire had not hurt them at all. It had not burned their hair or clothes. They did not smell like smoke.

Daniel 3:26-27

The king of Babylon made a law. The law said no one should say bad things about God. Only God could save men from fire.

Daniel 3:28-29

DANIEL AND THE LIONS' DEN

CHAPTER 43

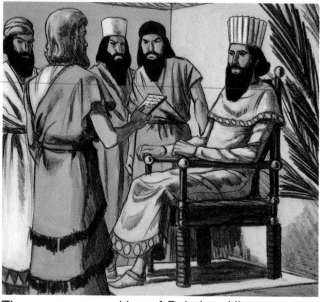

There was a new king of Babylon. His name was Darius. King Darius chose men to help him. Daniel was their leader. The other men did not like Daniel. They did not want him to be their leader.

Daniel 5:30-31; 6:1-5

The men knew Daniel prayed to God. They went to the king. They asked him to make a new law. The king made the new law. It said people could not pray to God. People who did not obey the law would be put in a lions' den. The lions would eat them.

Daniel 6:6-7

Daniel prayed to God three times a day. The wicked men saw Daniel praying. They told the king.

Daniel 6:10-13

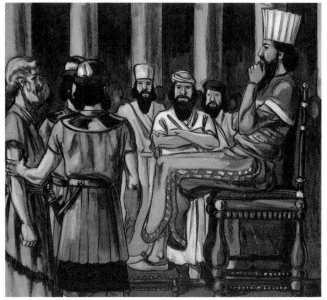

The king knew Daniel must be put in the lions' den. The king tried to think of a way to save him. But the law could not be changed. The king told his servants to put Daniel in the lions' den. King Darius told Daniel God would save him.

Daniel 6:14-16

The king fasted all night. He could not sleep.

Daniel 6:18

In the morning the king went to the lions' den. He called to Daniel. Daniel answered. The lions had not hurt him. He said God had shut the lions' mouths.

Daniel 6:19-22

The king was very happy. Daniel was safe because God had helped him.

Daniel 6:23-27

RETURN TO JERUSALEM

The Jews lived in Babylon for many years. Cyrus became the king. God told him to let the Jews build a new temple in Jerusalem. Cyrus told the Jews to go back to Jerusalem.

Ezra 1:1-3

The Jews went back to Jerusalem. They took gold and silver and beautiful dishes for the temple.

Ezra 1:4-11

The Jews built an altar and made sacrifices to God. They began to build the temple. They were happy. They prayed to God and thanked him.

Ezra 3:3-13

Some wicked men in Jerusalem were angry. They did not want the Jews to build a temple. They tried to stop them.

Ezra 4:1-5

But the Jews worked for a long time. At last the temple was finished.

Ezra 6:14-15

Ezra was a prophet of God. He lived in Babylon. Ezra went to Jerusalem to teach the Jews. He read all the commandments to the people. He told them to obey God's commandments and to repent. The people listened to him.

Ezra 7:6; Nehemiah 8:1-5, 8

Nehemiah was a prophet. He also went to Jerusalem.

Nehemiah 2:11-12

Nehemiah was sad when he got there. The wall around the city was broken down. The gates in the wall were burned. Nehemiah told the Jews they should build the wall and the gates again.

Nehemiah 2:17-18

The Jews began to build the wall. Wicked men tried to stop them. The Jews kept working. God blessed them. At last the wall and the gates were finished.

Nehemiah 2:19-20; 4:1-8; 6:15

Nehemiah talked to the people. He knew the Jews did not obey God's commandments. They were mean to each other. He told the Jews to be righteous.

Nehemiah 5:6-11

The Jews promised to obey God. They promised to keep the sabbath day holy. They promised to pay tithing. They promised to live good lives.

Nehemiah 9:38; 10:28-38

ESTHER

CHAPTER 45

Some Jews did not go back to Jerusalem. They stayed in Babylon. One of them was a beautiful girl named Esther.

Esther 2:5-7

Esther's father and mother were dead. She lived with her cousin Mordecai. Mordecai was a good man.

Esther 2:5-7

The king of the land gave a big feast. He asked many people to come.

Esther 1:5

The king sent for the queen to come to the feast. But she would not come. The king was angry. He said he would choose a new queen.

Esther 1:10-22

The king sent for many young women to come to his house. Esther went to the king's house.

Esther 2:2-4, 8

The king saw that Esther was beautiful. He loved her and chose her to be the queen.

Esther 2:17

Haman was one of the king's leaders. He hated the Jews. Haman made the people bow down to him. Mordecai would not bow down. Haman was angry.

Esther 3:1-5

Haman told the king the Jews would not obey the laws. Haman wanted to have the Jews killed. Letters were sent to leaders in the kingdom. The letters said all the Jews should be killed.

Esther 3:6-9, 13-15

The Jews heard about the letters. They were afraid and sad. They fasted and prayed for help.

Esther 4:3

Queen Esther heard about the letters. She sent a servant to ask Mordecai what had happened.

Esther 4:4-5

Mordecai said Esther would be killed because she was a Jew. Mordecai said Esther should try to save the Jews. Esther told all the Jews to fast for three days. She fasted, too. Then she went to the king.

Esther 4:7-16; 5:1

The king asked Esther what she wanted. He said she could have anything. Esther asked the king to come to a feast. She wanted Haman to come, too.

Esther 5:3-8

Esther told the king about Haman's plan to kill the Jews. She told him she was a Jew. The king was angry. He had Haman killed.

Esther 7:1-10

The king told Mordecai to write letters to all the kingdom. Mordecai told the Jews to kill anyone who tried to kill them.

Esther 8:8-11

The Jews were happy. Esther had saved them.

Esther 8:16-17

JOB

CHAPTER 46

Job was a very good man. He always did what was right. He obeyed God's commandments. Job was also a rich man. He had many animals and servants. He had a wife and ten children. God had given him many blessings.

Job 1:1-3

God knew Job was a righteous man. Satan also knew Job was righteous. Satan said Job was righteous because God had given him so many blessings. Satan said Job would not be righteous if his blessings were taken away.

Job 1:6-11

God said Satan could take away everything Job had. But Satan could not hurt Job. Then Satan would see that Job would still be righteous.

Job 1:12

One day four servants came to Job. They said all of Job's oxen and servants had been killed. They said a fire had burned all his sheep. They said his camels had been stolen.

Job 1:14-17

They said a strong wind blew down Job's son's house. All Job's children were killed. Job had nothing left.

Job 1:18-19

Job was very sad. But he was not angry at God. He fell to the ground and worshiped God. He said he had nothing when he was born. God gave him everything. Now God had taken it away. Job still loved God.

Job 1:20-22

God talked to Satan again. He said everything had been taken from Job. And Job was still righteous. But Satan said Job would not be righteous if he were very sick. So God said Satan could make Job sick. But Satan could not kill him.

Job 2:1-6

Job became very sick. His body was covered with sores. He wished he had not been born. Job's wife asked if he still believed God was good. Job said he did. Job said God gave people good things. God sometimes let bad things happen to them. Sometimes bad things happened to good people.

Job 2:7, 9-10; 3:1-13

Three of Job's friends came to see him. They were sorry for him. They told Job God punishes wicked people. They said God does not punish good people. The friends said Job must have been wicked. Bad things would not happen to him if he were righteous.

Job 2:11-13; 3-19

Job told his friends they were not helping him. He said he had not been wicked. He did not know why so many bad things had happened to him. Job still believed in God. Job said he might die. But he would always love God. If he did die, he would be resurrected. He would have his body again. He would see God.

Job 4-19

Again Job's friends told him he had been wicked. They said he may have taken things away from poor people. Or he may not have helped people when they needed help. They said God knows when people are wicked. No one can hide his sins from God. They told Job to repent. Then God would bless him.

Job 22

Job told his friends he was righteous. He said God knew he was not wicked. Job said some wicked people do not have troubles. And sometimes righteous people have many troubles. Job said he did not know why God had let bad things happen to him.

Job 26-28

Then Job heard the voice of God. God asked Job many questions. Where was Job when God made the world? What did Job know about the clouds, the snow, and the rain? What did Job know about the animals and the plants on the earth? God made these wonderful things.

Job 38, 39, 40:1

Job answered God. Job said he did not understand these things. God told Job men cannot always understand why God does things. Men must trust God no matter what happens to them.

Then Job saw God. Job had been righteous through all his troubles. Job loved God. He trusted God.

Job 40-42:6

God told Job's friends he was angry at them. The things they told Job were not right. God told them to bring animals for a sacrifice. Job prayed for his friends.

Job 42:7-10

God blessed Job. He gave Job more than he had before. God gave him more animals. Job and his wife had more children. They were happy. Job lived to be a very old man. He was very righteous.

Job 42:10-17

THE PROPHETS
TELL ABOUT JESUS

CHAPTER 47

Many of the people were not like Job. They were wicked. They did not obey God's commandments. They did not listen to his prophets.

Many prophets told the people to repent. They told the people that Jesus Christ would come to earth. He would be the Savior. He would die to save all the people on the earth.

1 Nephi 1:18-20

Some of the prophets who told about Jesus Christ were Moses, Jeremiah, Micah, Zechariah, Lehi, and Isaiah. The prophets said Jesus Christ would be born in Bethlehem. Jesus would grow up as other children do. People would not know he was the Son of God.

Jacob 7:11; Isaiah 7:14-15; 9:6; Micah 5:2

God would send a prophet to help Jesus. His name would be John. He would teach the people about Jesus. He would baptize Jesus. He would be called John the Baptist.

Isaiah 40:3; John 1:6; Matt. 3:1

Jesus would love everyone. He would do many miracles. He would teach men about God. He would show men how to be like Heavenly Father. He would suffer for their sins.

Isaiah 53:11-12; 61:1; Jeremiah 33:14-16

Some people would not believe in Jesus. They would hate him. They would crucify him on a cross. He would die and then be resurrected. The things the prophets said about Jesus did happen. The New Testament tells about the life of Jesus Christ.

Moses 7:55-56; Zechariah 13:6; Isaiah 53:5

AFTER THE OLD TESTAMENT

CHAPTER 48

The Old Testament prophets died. Four hundred years went by. Most of the Jews did not obey God.

Armies from other lands captured the Jews. Wicked kings from other lands made them slaves. The kings killed thousands of them.

The kings would not let the Jews make sacrifices to God. They took the things made of gold from the temple. The kings worshiped idols in the temple.

The last army to capture the Jews was the Roman army. The Romans broke down the walls of Jerusalem. They captured the city. They sent a man named Herod to be the king of the Jews.

Herod wanted the Jews to like him. So he made the temple beautiful again. He had thousands of men work on it. They put gold and silver back into the temple. When it was finished it was very beautiful. But the Jews still did not like Herod.

Herod was very wicked. He killed many people. He killed his wife and two sons. He tried to kill the baby Jesus.

The Jews did not want Herod to be their king. They did not want the Romans to be their leaders. The Jews were waiting for the Savior to come. They thought he would help them fight the Romans. They thought the Savior would be their king.

WORDS TO KNOW

A

altar People pray at an <u>altar.</u> People burned animals on an <u>altar.</u>

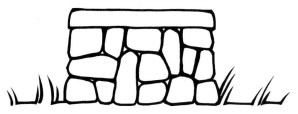

angel <u>An angel</u> is one of <u>God's helpers.</u> An <u>angel</u> comes from heaven.
<u>An angel</u> talked to Adam.

anoint To <u>anoint</u> means to <u>put oil on</u> someone's head and bless him.

anointed Samuel <u>anointed</u> Saul to be king of Israel.

ark An <u>ark</u> keeps things safe inside it. One kind of <u>ark</u> is a <u>big ship.</u>
Noah took animals on <u>the ark.</u>

ark of the covenant <u>The ark of the covenant</u> was <u>a box.</u> The two stones with the Ten Commandments written on them were kept in this box.

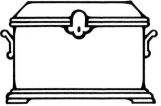

army Men in an <u>army</u> fight other men.

armies Two <u>armies</u> went to fight each other.

B

baptized When we join the church, we <u>are baptized.</u>
When we <u>are baptized,</u> we are <u>put under the water and brought up out of the water.</u>

barley <u>Barley</u> is a plant like grass. It has seeds on it.
<u>Barley</u> seeds are sometimes used to make bread.

barrel <u>The barrel</u> was full of water.

basket Moses' mother put him in a basket.

battle A battle is a big fight.

beat The man beat the boy with a stick.
The man hit the boy with a stick.

beating Moses saw a man beating an Israelite.

beautiful Something nice to look at is beautiful.
The girl was beautiful. The dishes were beautiful.
The garden was beautiful.

believe To believe means to think something is true.

believed The people believed what Elijah said.
The people thought what Elijah said was true.

blessed God blessed Jacob.
God helped Jacob and gave him good things.

blessing Jacob gave his sons a blessing.
Jacob put his hands on his sons' heads and prayed for his sons.

birthright blessing Long ago people gave the birthright blessing to the oldest son. It was the best blessing.
Isaac did not give Esau the birthright blessing.

bow Haman made the people bow to him.

bull Elijah put the bull on the altar.

bury When people die, we bury them.
Bible people put them in caves.

buried David was buried in Jerusalem.

C

calf A calf is a cow's baby.

camel A camel is an animal.

candlesticks Candlesticks lighted the temple.

captain A captain is a leader.
The captain of the ship did not want to throw Jonah in the sea.

captured The Israelites captured the city.
The Israelites took the city away from the people who lived there.
The Jews were captured.
The Jews were taken away from their land by the people of Babylon.

cave Elijah hid in a cave.

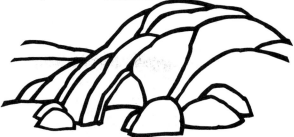

choose God lets us choose to do good things or to do bad things.
We should choose to do good things.

chose God chose David to be king.
God picked David to be king.

chosen David was chosen to be king.

commandments Commandments are things God tells people to do.
Good people obey God's commandments.
Good people do what God tells them to do.

crucify To <u>crucify</u> means to <u>kill</u> someone by <u>putting</u> him on a <u>cross</u>.

crucified Jesus was <u>crucified</u> on a cross.

curtains The tabernacle had a wall of <u>curtains</u>.

D

daughter A <u>daughter</u> is the girl in a family.
The king's <u>daughter</u> found Moses.

den <u>A den</u> is a place where wild animals live.

destroy To <u>destroy</u> means to <u>burn</u> or <u>tear down</u>.

destroyed The city of Jerusalem was <u>destroyed</u>.

divided The Red Sea <u>was divided</u>.
The 12 tribes <u>were divided</u>.

E

earrings People wore <u>earrings</u> made of gold.

earthquake <u>An earthquake</u> makes the earth move and break.
<u>The earthquake</u> broke down the walls.

elders <u>Elders</u> are men who help in the Church.
<u>Elders</u> have the priesthood.

enough The Israelites had <u>enough</u> manna to eat.
The Israelites had <u>as much manna as they needed</u>.

escape To <u>escape</u> means to <u>get away</u> from someone.

escaped The Israelites <u>escaped</u> from the Egyptians.

evil <u>Evil</u> is something bad.
Satan is <u>evil</u>. Telling lies is <u>evil</u>. People who do <u>very bad things</u> are <u>evil</u>.

F

faith To have <u>faith</u> is to believe something is true.
We should have <u>faith</u> in God.
We must <u>have faith in</u> Jesus Christ.
We must <u>believe and obey</u> Jesus Christ.

famine A famine is having <u>no food</u>.

There was a <u>famine</u> in Canaan. There was <u>no food</u> in Canaan.

fasted Moses <u>fasted</u> for 40 days.
Moses <u>did not eat or drink</u> for 40 days.

flesh-and-blood bodies We have <u>flesh-and-blood bodies</u> now. Before we came to earth we did not have <u>flesh-and-blood bodies</u>. We had spirit bodies.

flood Noah saved the animals from the flood. The flood was water that covered the earth.

forgive To forgive someone means to forget the bad things that he has done.
Jesus Christ will forgive us for the bad things we do if we are sorry and stop doing them.

forgave God forgave the people of Israel.
God forgot the bad things the people of Israel did.

furnace A furnace has fire in it.
The king had a big furnace.

G

garden A garden has trees, flowers and grass.
Adam and Eve lived in the Garden of Eden.

giant A giant is a very tall, strong man.
Goliath was a giant.

gift A gift is a present.
It is something that is given to someone.
The king gave Abraham a gift.

gospel The gospel is what Jesus teaches us to do.
We believe in the gospel of Jesus Christ.

H

heal To heal is to make a sick person well.
God helped Elisha heal people.

healed Elisha healed the sick man.

husband A husband is a man who is married.
Father is mother's husband.
Abraham was Sarah's husband.

I

idol An idol is a statue.
Some people prayed to an idol. They did not pray to God.

J

jar A jar holds oil or water.

judge A judge is a leader. The judges helped people to know what to do.
A judge says what is good and what is bad.
To judge is to say what is good or what is bad.

K

kingdom A kingdom is a land that has a king for a leader.
Rehoboam was the king of the kingdom of Judah.

L

language The words we use to talk or write to other people are called language.
God changed the language of the people. They could not understand each other.

lead To lead means to show people what to do.
God told Moses to lead the Israelites.

leader Moses was the leader of the Israelites.

leper A leper is a sick person with sores all over his body.
Naaman was a leper.

lice Lice are very small bugs that bite.
The lice bit the people of Egypt.

lies Lies are not true.
Potiphar's wife told lies about Joseph.
Potiphar's wife said things about Joseph that were not true.

M

married Isaac married Rebekah.
Isaac was Rebekah's husband. Rebekah was Isaac's wife.

miracle A miracle is something that shows the power of God.
God helps prophets to do miracles.

mountain Moses went up on the mountain.

O

obey To obey means to do what we are told to do.

obeyed Enoch obeyed God.
Enoch did what God told him to do.

P

pottage Pottage is thick soup.
Esau ate the pottage.

power God has great power.
God can do things people cannot do. God can do everything.

pray To pray means to talk with God.
I pray to God every day.

prayed Hannah prayed to God to give her a son.

priesthood The priesthood is the power of God.
Samuel had the priesthood.
Samuel had the power of God.

priests Priests have the priesthood. Priests are men who help in the Church.
The priests helped in the temple.

prison A prison is a place where people are put and cannot get out.
Joseph was put in prison.

promise To promise is to say we will do something.
We promise to obey God.

promised God promised to bless Abraham.
He gave Abraham the promised land.

prophet God speaks to a prophet.
A prophet tells us what God wants us to know.
Elijah was a prophet.

punished We are punished when we do something bad. Sad things happen to us when we are punished.

Q

quails Quails are birds.

179

R

rainbow God put <u>a rainbow</u> in the sky.

ram <u>A ram</u> is a sheep.
Abraham saw <u>a ram</u>.

repent If we do something bad, we should <u>repent</u>.
If we do something bad, we should <u>feel sorry and not do it again</u>.

repented The people of Nineveh <u>repented</u>.

resurrected Jesus Christ was <u>resurrected</u>. His <u>spirit came back to his body</u>.
He is alive. He will never die again.

righteous To be <u>righteous</u> means to <u>do what is right</u>.
<u>Righteous</u> people <u>obey God's commandments</u>.

rod A <u>rod</u> is a <u>stick</u>.

S

sabbath The <u>sabbath</u> is the <u>day we go to Church</u>.
We should not work on <u>the sabbath</u>.

sacrifice God told men to <u>sacrifice</u> animals.

sacrificed Abraham <u>sacrificed</u> an animal.
Abraham <u>killed</u> an animal. He <u>burned</u> it <u>on an altar</u>.

Jesus <u>sacrificed</u> his life for us. He died on the cross.
Jesus <u>gave</u> his life for us.

save Jesus died to <u>save</u> us.
Jesus died so we <u>could live with Heavenly Father</u> again.

servant <u>A servant</u> works for someone else.

servants Potiphar had many <u>servants.</u>
Potiphar had many <u>people who worked for him</u>.

shepherd <u>A shepherd</u> takes care of sheep.
David was <u>a shepherd</u> when he was a boy.
David <u>took care of sheep</u> when he was a boy.

slaves <u>Slaves</u> are people who are <u>made to work</u> for other people.
The king made his <u>slaves</u> work hard.

sling <u>A sling</u> is used to throw stones.
David used <u>a sling</u> to throw a stone at Goliath.

soldiers Soldiers fight in an army.

spies Joshua sent spies into the promised land. Joshua sent men into the promised land to see what it was like.

spirit bodies Spirit bodies look like flesh-and-blood bodies.

spirits We were spirits when we lived in heaven with God.
We did not have flesh-and-blood bodies then.

store To store something means to keep it until it is needed.

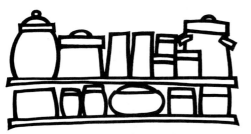

stored The Egyptians stored food.

swallow We swallow food. It goes down our throats.

swallowed A big fish swallowed Jonah.

sword David killed Goliath with a sword.

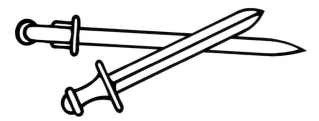

suffer We suffer when our bodies hurt.
We suffer when we feel very sad.

suffered Jesus suffered for us.

T

tabernacle A tabernacle is a place to pray to God. God told Moses to build a tabernacle.
The Israelites had a tabernacle. It was like a tent.

teach To teach means to help someone learn. Enoch wanted to teach the people.

taught Enoch taught the people God's commandments.

temple A temple is God's house.
We do God's work in a temple.
Solomon's temple had stone walls.

tested To be tested is to show if we will do what is right.
God put us on earth to be tested.

thirsty To be thirsty is to want a drink of water. The Israelites had no water. They were thirsty.

tithing God gave us everything we have. Tithing is what we give back to him.
Abraham paid tithing.

travel To travel means to go from one place to another.

traveled The Israelites traveled from Egypt to the promised land.

tribe A tribe is many people.

tribes The families of Jacob's 12 sons were called tribes.

trouble Trouble is something bad that happens to us.

troubles Job had many troubles.

trusted Potiphar trusted Joseph.
Potiphar knew that Joseph would do what he should do.

V

vision A vision is a dream from God.
Enoch saw Jesus Christ in a vision.

W

well A <u>well</u> is a <u>deep hole with water in it.</u>
Rachel came to <u>the well</u> to get water.

wheat <u>Wheat</u> is a <u>plant</u> with small seeds.
We use <u>wheat</u> seeds to make bread.

wicked <u>Wicked</u> means <u>very bad.</u>
<u>Wicked</u> people do <u>bad things.</u> They <u>do not obey
God.</u>

wilderness <u>A wilderness</u> is a place where there
are <u>no cities or people.</u>
Moses and the Israelites lived in <u>the wilderness</u>
for 40 years.

wise God made Solomon <u>wise.</u> God helped him
<u>know what was true.</u> Solomon knew how to help
people.

wisest Solomon was <u>the wisest</u> man on earth.

worship To <u>worship</u> means to <u>show God we
love him.</u>
We <u>worship</u> God by <u>obeying his commandments.</u>
We <u>worship</u> God by <u>praying to him.</u>

Y

yard <u>A yard</u> is the land around a building.
There was <u>a yard</u> around the tabernacle.

young A child is <u>young.</u> My grandmother is old.
David was <u>young</u> when he killed Goliath.

youngest David had older brothers. David was
the <u>youngest</u> son of Jesse.

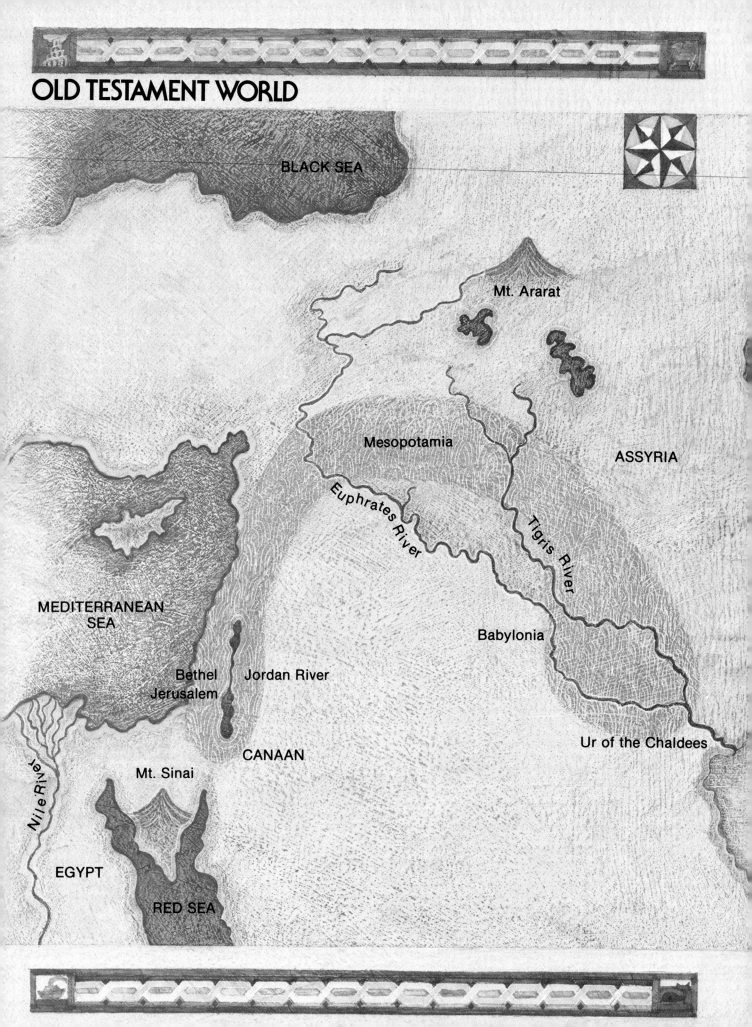

OLD TESTAMENT WORLD

BLACK SEA

Mt. Ararat

Mesopotamia

ASSYRIA

Euphrates River

Tigris River

MEDITERRANEAN
SEA

Babylonia

Bethel
Jerusalem

Jordan River

Ur of the Chaldees

CANAAN

Mt. Sinai

Nile River

EGYPT

RED SEA

PLACES TO KNOW

America America is the land where the Jaredites went when they left the Tower of Babel. Lehi's family left Jerusalem and went to America.

Babylon Babylon was a land near the promised land. An army from Babylon captured the Kingdom of Judah and made the people slaves.

Bethlehem Bethlehem was a city in the promised land. David grew up in Bethlehem.

Canaan Canaan was the land where Jacob lived. It was the promised land. Later the Israelites captured Canaan. Then they called it Israel.

earth Earth is the place where we live now. Jesus made the earth.

Egypt Egypt was the land where the Israelites were slaves. Moses led the Israelites out of Egypt.

Garden of Eden The Garden of Eden was a beautiful garden with trees and flowers. Adam and Eve lived there before they ate fruit from the tree of good and evil.

heaven Heaven is where Heavenly Father lives. We lived in heaven before we came to earth.

Israel Israel was the land where the Israelites lived. It was the promised land. It was called Canaan before the Israelites captured it.

Jericho Jericho was a city in the promised land. Joshua and the Israelites captured Jericho.

Jerusalem Jerusalem was a city in the promised land. King Solomon built a temple in Jerusalem.

Jordan River Joshua led the Israelites across the Jordan River into the promised land.

Kingdom of Israel The Kingdom of Israel was the north part of the promised land. Ten tribes of Israel lived there.

Kingdom of Judah The kingdom of Judah was the south part of the promised land. Two tribes of Israel lived there. They were called Jews.

Moab Moab was the land where Naomi's son married Ruth.

Mount Sinai Mount Sinai was the mountain where Jesus gave the Ten Commandments to Moses.

Nineveh Nineveh was a city where wicked people lived. God sent Jonah to tell them to repent.

promised land The promised land was the land God promised to Abraham's family. Joshua led the Israelites into the promised land.

Red Sea Moses led the Israelites through the Red Sea after they left Egypt.

Ur Ur was a city where Abraham lived. Many people in Ur worshiped idols.

Zion Zion was the city where Enoch was the prophet. God took all the people in Zion to heaven.

PEOPLE TO KNOW

Aaron Aaron was Moses' brother. He helped Moses lead the Israelites back to the promised land.

Abednego Abednego was a righteous Jew and a friend of Daniel. Jesus saved him from burning in the furnace.

Abel Abel was a righteous son of Adam and Eve. Abel's brother Cain killed him.

Abraham Abraham was blessed by Jesus. Jesus gave him the promised land. Abraham's family would have the priesthood.

Adam Adam was the first man on earth. He walked and talked with God.

Ahab Ahab was a wicked king of Israel. Jezebel was his wife.

Baal Baal was an idol. Many wicked people worshiped Baal.

Bathsheba Bathsheba was Uriah's wife. King David married Bathsheba after Uriah was killed.

Boaz Boaz was a righteous man in Bethlehem. He married Ruth.

Cain Cain was a wicked son of Adam and Eve. He killed his brother Abel.

Cyrus Cyrus was a king. He let the Jews go back to Jerusalem from Babylon.

Daniel Daniel was a righteous Jew. God kept him safe in the lions' den.

Darius Darius was a king of Babylon. He did not want Daniel to be hurt in the lions' den.

David David killed Goliath. David was a king of Israel.

devil The devil is a spirit son of Heavenly Father. He would not obey Heavenly Father. Heavenly Father sent him out of heaven. The devil is called Lucifer or Satan.

Egyptians The Egyptians were people who lived in Egypt.

Eli Eli was an Israelite judge. Samuel helped him take care of the Tabernacle.

Elijah Elijah was a prophet. He showed the priests of Baal that God has great power.

Elisha Elisha was the prophet after Elijah. God helped Elisha do many miracles.

Enoch Enoch was a prophet. God took Enoch and his people to heaven.

Esau Esau was the older son of Isaac and Rebekah. He let his brother Jacob have the birthright blessing.

Esther Esther was a Jew. She became a queen in Babylon. She saved her people's lives.

Eve Eve was the first woman on earth. She was Adam's wife.

Ezra Ezra was a prophet. He taught the Jews when they came back to Jerusalem.

God Heavenly Father, Jesus Christ and the Holy Ghost are all called God. They all have great powers.

Goliath Goliath was a Philistine giant. He was killed by David.

Haman Haman was a leader for the king in Babylon. He wanted to kill all the Jews. Esther stopped him.

Hannah Hannah was a righteous woman. She was Samuel's mother.

Heavenly Father Heavenly Father is the father of our spirit bodies. He lives in heaven. We pray to Heavenly Father. Sometimes we call Heavenly Father God.

Holy Ghost The Holy Ghost works with Heavenly Father and Jesus. He helps people know the truth. The Holy Ghost has a spirit body. He does not have a flesh-and-bone body.

Isaac Isaac was the righteous son of Abraham and Sarah. He was the father of Jacob and Esau.

Isaiah Isaiah was a prophet. He told the people about Jesus.

Israel Jacob's name was changed to Israel. He was the righteous son of Isaac. Israel had 12 sons.

Israel The families of Jacob's 12 sons were called the people of Israel. They were the 12 tribes of Israel.

Israelites The families of Jacob's 12 sons were called Israelites. They were the 12 tribes of Israel.

Jacob Jacob was the righteous son of Isaac. Jacob had 12 sons. Jesus changed Jacob's name to Israel.

Jaredites The Jaredites were people who followed Jared and his brother. God led them from the Tower of Babel to America.

Jeremiah Jeremiah was a prophet. He told the people about Jesus Christ.

Jeroboam Jeroboam was a wicked king of the Kingdom of Israel.

Jesse Jesse was the father of King David. Jesse lived in Bethlehem.

Jesus Jesus is our Savior. He is the son of Heavenly Father. Sometimes we call Jesus God.

Jews The Jews were Israelites who lived in the Kingdom of Judah.

Jezebel Jezebel was King Ahab's wife. She wanted to kill Elijah.

Job Job was a righteous man. He had many troubles, but he still loved God.

Jonah Jonah was a prophet. A big fish swallowed him. Jonah taught the people in Nineveh.

Joseph Joseph was a righteous son of Jacob and Rachel. His brothers sold him. He became a leader in Egypt.

Joshua Joshua was the prophet after Moses. He helped the Israelites capture the promised land.

Laban Laban was the father of Leah and Rachel.

Leah Leah was a daughter of Laban. She married Jacob.

Lehi Lehi was a prophet in Jerusalem. God told him to leave Jerusalem. Lehi's family went to America.

Lucifer Lucifer is a spirit son of Heavenly Father. He would not obey Heavenly Father. Heavenly Father sent him out of heaven. Lucifer is called Satan or the devil.

Melchizedek Melchizedek was a righteous king. He had the priesthood. Abraham paid tithing to him.

Meshach Meshach was a righteous Jew and a friend of Daniel. Jesus saved him from burning in the furnace.

Micah Micah was a prophet. He told the people about Jesus.

Miriam Miriam was Moses' sister.

Mordecai Mordecai was a righteous Jew. He was Esther's cousin.

Moses Moses was a prophet. He led the Israelites out of Egypt. He took them back to the promised land.

Naaman Naaman was a leper. God helped Elisha heal Naaman.

Naomi Naomi was a righteous woman. One of her sons married Ruth.

Nathan Nathan was a prophet. He talked to King David.

Nehemiah Nehemiah was a prophet when the Jews came back to Jerusalem. He helped them build the wall again.

Noah Noah was a righteous man. He built an ark. His family was saved when the flood came.

Obed Obed was the son of Boaz and Ruth. He was King David's grandfather.

Orpah Orpah married one of Naomi's sons.

Philistines The Philistines were people who fought the Israelites. Goliath was a Philistine.

Potiphar Potiphar was a soldier for the king of Egypt. Joseph worked for Potiphar.

Rachel Rachel was a daughter of Laban. She was Jacob's wife and Joseph's mother.

Rebekah Rebekah was Isaac's wife. She was the mother of Jacob and Esau.

Rehoboam Rehoboam was one of Solomon's sons. He was a wicked king of the Kingdom of Judah.

Ruth Ruth married one of Naomi's sons. After he died, Ruth married Boaz.

Samuel Samuel was a prophet. He was an Israelite judge. He anointed King Saul and King David.

Sarah Sarah was Abraham's wife. She was Isaac's mother.

Satan Satan is a spirit son of Heavenly Father. He would not obey Heavenly Father. Heavenly Father sent him out of heaven. Satan is called Lucifer or the devil.

Saul Saul was the first king of Israel.

Seth Seth was a righteous son of Adam and Eve.

Shadrach Shadrach was a righteous Jew and a friend of Daniel. Jesus saved him from burning in the furnace.

Solomon Solomon was the son of King David and Bathsheba. He became king of Israel and built a temple.

Uriah Uriah was Bathsheba's husband. King David had him killed in a battle.

Zechariah Zechariah was a prophet. He told the people about Jesus.

OLD TESTAMENT EVENTS

4000 B.C.
Adam and Eve
in the Garden of Eden

3000 B.C.
Enoch and his city
taken to heaven

2400 B.C.
Noah and the Flood

1571 B.C.
Moses' journey in
Sinai wilderness

1451 B.C.
Joshua enters
the Promised Land

1047 B.C.
David and the united
Kingdom of Israel

1015 B.C.
Solomon's temple
in Jerusalem

2200 B.C.	1996 B.C.	1836 B.C.	1745 B.C.
Tower of Babel	Abraham in Ur, Egypt,	Jacob and the twelve tribes	Joseph in Egypt
in Babylonia	and Canaan	of Israel in the Promised Land	

975 B.C.	721 B.C.	587 B.C.	537
Divided Israel	Northern Kingdom	Judah taken captive	Judah returns and
	taken away and lost	to Babylon	rebuilds the temple

Your comments and suggestions about this book are appreciated. Please submit them to—

Curriculum Planning and Development
Floor 24
50 East North Temple Street
Salt Lake City, Utah 84150
USA

Identify yourself by name, address, ward, and stake. Then identify the name of the manual, how you used it, your feelings regarding its strengths and weaknesses, and any recommended improvements.